Hurt by My Father

HEALED BY GOD

Hurt by My Father

HEALED BY GOD

C. Joyce Farrar-Rosemon

WINNER AT LIFE PUBLISHERS
ATLANTA, GEORGIA 30281
WWW.WOMENSEMPOWERMENTSEMINARS.COM
404-202-8776

Hurt by My Father HEALED BY GOD

Printed in the United States of America November 2015

ISBN-10: 0985626232

ISBN-13: 978-0-9856262-3-5

Cover and Interior Design by Donna Osborn Clark at www.CreationByDonna.com

WINNER AT LIFE PUBLISHERS
ATLANTA, GEORGIA 30281
WWW.WOMENSEMPOWERMENTSEMINARS.COM
404-202-8776

IN MEMORIAM

To Tiffany, my stillborn daughter:
Your death brought a resurrection and a desire
to seek that place of Shalom in my spirit.
Thank you for being a ministering angel in my life.
(Hebrews 1:13-14)

ACKNOWLEDGMENTS

First, and foremost I thank God for giving me the vision, insight, and the ability to write this book. In addition, I thank God for favoring and affirming me as the apple of his eye. His goodness and mercy have always followed me.

Secondly, I want to thank the individuals featured in this anthology who have shared their stories with me personally or in printed form. They have been irons that have sharpened my perception of God's ability to resurrect, empower, and heal all types of hurts and heartaches.

Lastly, I want to thank my husband Tillmon, son David, family, friends, supporters, and members of the Wesley Chapel Creative Writers Group in Decatur, Georgia for their encouragement and support of my vision "to set at liberty the bruised and broken-hearted."

INTRODUCTION

We were under great pressure, far beyond our ability to endure, so that we despaired of life itself. Indeed, we felt we had received the sentence of death. But this happened that we might not rely on ourselves but on God, who raises the dead. II Corinthians 4:8-9 NIV

How do you move forward in relationships when you have given all you can give and the last two words you hear from your lover is, *Goodbye bitch*? Better yet, what chance do you have in life when at the age of 3 months, half-dead and bleeding from your navel your mom gives you away for a pair of shoes? What hope do you have in life as a Christian believer when you are excommunicated from your church for being labeled the *Spawn of Satan*? Other individuals in this anthology were given the titles of *Homosexual Addict*, *Jesus Killer*, and many were left to feel like no one loved them. Somehow we, myself included, not only survived, but overcame and flourished in life. Our stories are told within the pages of this book so that you too can overcome any hurts you may be experiencing now or from the past.

Hurt by My Father, Healed by God, is a compilation of true life accounts of individuals who have been hurt by someone in a position of authority over them. The person(s) that violated them may have been a parent, relative, friend, minister, doctor, or even a politician. Included as well are egregious patriarchal institutions or laws that support discrimination, sexism, racism, genocide, as well as gender based violence against women. What all the respondents have in common is that someone who was close to them or who was an authority figure and should have protected them instead abused and violated them. Most importantly, the aim of this book is to show how these individuals regardless of their background, nationality, age, race, or gender, were healed by God.

The common denominator these individuals share is that what was meant to destroy them instead caused them to rise up out of the ashes like the mythical phoenix and triumph over their enemies. What all the overcomers—and I choose to call them *overcomers*, rather than *victims or survivors*,– agree upon is that it was only through the miraculous power of God that they were set free from a past that could have scarred them for life or led to a premature death.

As a trained psychotherapist I have counseled with and have seen significant strives with individuals who have been deeply bruised and violated by authority figures. I wholeheartedly endorse professional counseling from a licensed therapist, but I am also aware of the limitations of therapy. Some of the wounds that individuals and groups have suffered are so deep, unconscionable, and traumatic, that it is only through the grace of God that some of the featured overcomers in this book have gone on to achieve, thrive, and become contributing citizens of society.

Editors, Allen C. Sherman PhD and Thomas G. Plante PhD, in their book, *Faith and Health: Psychological Perspectives* (2001) document empirical studies that have shown that chronic anger and hostility have been found to adversely affect one's health and contribute to poor cardiovascular performance and decreased functioning of the immune system. These studies also found that these reactions have been associated with health compromising behaviors and conditions such as high blood pressure, depression, increased substance abuse, and general poor health status.

Their scientific studies attest to the age old Biblical wisdom found in Proverbs 15:13, "A merry heart maketh a cheerful countenance: but by sorrow of the heart the spirit [one's life] is broken." Our bodies are not designed to hold in bitterness, pain, unforgiveness, aggression, and anger. The obvious question arises as follows— how do we move on and live long, enjoyable lives, free of antidepressants, painkillers, drugs, addictions, dysfunctional behavior, and sleep medications?

I submit that we must first *confront the hurts of our past, forgive our abusers, and if necessary ourselves*, if we want to seize hold of a peaceful countenance. In some situations, due to the depravity and inhumanity of various acts, I propose that it will only be through the grace and power of God that those abused will ever be able to forgive their trespassers.

In this collection of accounts, respondents whose stories are not public were given the opportunity to remain anonymous. Most chose to have their identities made public. Please note that the identities of individuals who are family members, friends, or co-workers have been changed to protect their privacy unless this has also been disclosed publicly by some of the featured individuals.

As you read their stories, some will appear very controversial. You may take offense for example and adamantly disagree that an individual can be healed from homosexuality or drug addiction. Please note that *I am simply the messenger*. I have told their stories as anecdotal accounts—these are their unsolicited stories, based on their belief systems. Neither is this undertaking based on empirical research that has been submitted to peer review. They are simply anecdotal accounts from individuals who attribute their transformations to the power of God working in their lives.

Personally, I believe that their accounts are credible; otherwise I would not have included them in this anthology. As a Christian, Motivational Speaker, Certified Educator, and trained psychotherapist my purpose in writing is to share in written format, accounts of God's transformative power in the lives of believers as well as in my own life.

The world we live in today is plagued with violence and immorality. Anything goes as long as you can get the right attorney to successfully defend you in court. Individualism has replaced honesty, fairness, self-control, decency, justice, and in some cases God's word. The standard of what is right and wrong has been replaced with affluenza and/or what is legally defensible or politically correct. Our children are inheriting a world where there is no clear definition of what is right or wrong. Someone must come forth, lift up an enduring standard of justice and truth that will stand the test of time for eternity.

This is my attempt to be the canary in the mine and sound the alarm for a better world for our children who someday will become tomorrow's leaders, policy makers, and citizens of the world. The charge will be left to them to possess, replenish, establish standards of what is right and wrong, and make the Earth fruitful. I am well aware that there are different philosophical positions concerning morality espoused by different cultures and religions. My personal reference is found in allegiance to Biblical principles. I personally believe in its power to transform the hearts, minds, and lives of those who submit to the word of God *all over the world.* I know of no greater power in heaven or on earth that is able to bring together in love and unity people from every nation, tribe, and gender under the sun.

With that in mind, I willingly share these stories of other like-minded individuals who believe in the power of God to heal all manner of pain, diseases, and illnesses. As you read their triumphant accounts, and if you see yourself reflected in their lives, know that there is this same *healing balm in Gilead* that can release you from any pain, addiction, resentment, or unforgiveness that you may have harboring in your heart.

If you have tried counseling, and it has not worked, I appeal to you to drink from the living waters Jesus spoke about that will cause you to never thirst again. His promise to the woman at the well that had been involved in six failed relationships was that he would make her whole. I believe that you too, regardless of what you may have experienced in life, can be made whole again just like the individuals featured in this collection. I dare you to taste and you too will see that the Lord is good and that his mercies endure forever for all generations!

Table of Contents

Chapter 1

Tracy, the "Goodbye Bitch!" Healed from Lesbianism

On a sunny spring day I received a telephone call from a professional 35 year old woman named Tracy who wanted to sell her new townhouse in Atlanta. She asked whether I could represent her as the listing real estate broker. At that time I was a multimillion dollar Realtor and the qualifying broker of the firm that both my husband and I co-owned. After telling her "yes", Tracy and I agreed to meet later at her townhouse which was in a new subdivision that was still under construction.

At the townhouse we introduced ourselves and talked outside as we waited for Tracy's ex-partner, Nicole, to leave the house. While we waited Tracy explained that she had never lived in the house and had bought it brand new for Nicole at a cost of close to a quarter of a million dollars. Tracy told me that it was the last thing she had to do after terminating her toxic relationship with Nicole. Tracy emphasized that she had left the gay lifestyle with God's help and now had to rid herself of this monthly mortgage payment. She shared that she could not afford to pay two mortgages, this one and her other house out of state.

I was a little surprised by Tracy's pronouncement because her appearance did not look like she had completely made a full transition. Her outward show was ambiguous and appeared as if she could pass for someone straight or gay. Her pretty ebony skin was flawless without the help of makeup. Although she looked somewhat androgynous in her jeans and top, she still had a shapely feminine figure.

After about 10 minutes Nicole, a strikingly attractive young African-American woman emerged from the townhouse, got in her Mercedes convertible and left without an exchange of words with Tracy. Nicole could have easily passed for someone in her mid to late 20s. She wreaked sex appeal and did not seem to have a hint of homosexuality in her. Nicole permeated self-confidence and I'm sure she was used to not only men, but women taking double takes when she walked by.

We then entered the house and because Tracy was so forthright and in obvious pain, I asked what had happened as we toured the townhouse and viewed its many amenities and accoutrements. Tracy explained that she had taken on the traditional superior male role in her relationship with her former partner. Nicole had shared with Tracy that she had been hurt by her father, and in relationships with both men and women. Tracy revealed to Nicole that she was in the same boat and had been hurt by her father and a boyfriend in her teens. This was the initial bond that brought them together- their similar past of being mistreated and abused by men. Tracy wanted Nicole to feel safe in her arms and decided to honor her commitment by buying Nicole a brand new townhouse and agreeing to pay the mortgage and utilities for her.

Both agreed that they would have a long distance relationship with each other, and that when Tracy came to Atlanta, she would stay with Nicole. Tracy explained that she didn't want money, sex, or closeness. Her hope was that just the two of them would give each other love and that both would feel safe. In exchange for the house and commitment to keep her safe, Tracy thought that Nicole would mirror and give her love in return, which unfortunately did not happen.

After touring the house and signing the listing agreement, I shared with Tracy what I did outside of being a real estate broker. I told Tracy that I was an author of several self-help books and that it was uncanny that she called me to list her townhouse out of all the thousands of agents in Atlanta, and that we also shared this conversation. I explained to Tracy that I was working on a book about individuals who had been hurt by those in authority and had been healed by God. I asked whether I could include her story anonymously and she readily agreed hoping that it would help someone else who might want to leave the gay lifestyle behind them.

In subsequent interviews with Tracy she shared the following about her early years, familial, and close relationships with both men and women. Tracy was born and reared in the Midwest with her single mom and two brothers. She explained that she had a tumultuous beginning in utero. Unwanted by her biological father, he used to beat her mother regularly in the pelvic region in an attempt to abort Tracy. Her relatives were amazed that she was normal at delivery and were surprised that Tracy was not damaged in some way because of the brutality of her dad's beatings. As a result, Tracy told me that she developed a hatred for men in authority early in life.

Abandoned by her father, Tracy's mom, a very religious woman, took on the role of being both mother and father to Tracy and her two brothers. Tracy's relationship with her siblings and mother has always been a close one. In the eighth grade Tracy received a scholarship and was able to go to a private school and later graduated from college.

Her brother Rodney however, was challenged academically and instead of attending college fell prey to the harsh streets of Detroit, Michigan. By the time he reached adulthood he was an alcoholic. Once while intoxicated, Rodney was involved in a car accident which resulted in an embolism that required hospitalization for seven months. Tracy feared that she had lost him, but her brother survived this ordeal. However, months later he died from the effects of the car accident. Tracy's remaining brother Chris is presently battling drugs and has been caught up in the revolving door of the penal system.

In spite of Tracy's horrific beginning, during her teens she developed heterosexual relationships with males. After a failed relationship with one boyfriend during college who cheated on her, she turned away from men.

Nicole was not Tracy's first lesbian relationship. She had other relationships with women but the attachment was not as deep as it was with Nicole. They met at a gay party and continued to communicate with one another. At some point they decided to form a partnership which consummated in Tracy agreeing to buy Nicole a house to prove her love and fidelity towards Nicole.

Tracy drove to Atlanta during her Christmas vacation to close on the townhouse. After the settlement, Tracy realized she had made a huge mistake. Back at the house Nicole told her that she did not want Tracy to stay and preferred that she return to Michigan. Fortunately, for Tracy the townhouse was only in her name and Nicole did not have title or claim to the property. A fight ensued and Nicole pushed Tracy down the steps. Nicole took her to the emergency room and a cast was put on Tracy's driving foot. To Tracy's chagrin she had no choice but to drive back to Michigan in the snow with a cast on her foot.

An attempt was made during the next few months to salvage the relationship, but to no avail. Tracy made visits to Atlanta and Nicole also went to Michigan. On one return trip from Michigan, Tracy almost lost her life at the hands of her former partner who was driving. The two of them were discussing Tracy's insistence on ending the relationship. Nicole adamantly objected and endeavored to run the car off the road in an attempt to kill both of them. Fortunately, Tracy regained control of the car and prevented an accident.

Tracy then returned to Michigan with the full knowledge that this life-threatening encounter was indisputable confirmation that their relationship was over. Attempts to sell the townhouse proved fruitless due to the recession. Tracy called Nicole a few months later and told her she had to move because the house was going into foreclosure. Tracy told Nicole that she could no longer take care of her. Nicole resisted and Tracy eventually took her to court and got a judgment against her to move. However, Tracy's heart softened and she refused to put Nicole out.

Months later when the lights were turned off, Nicole called in anger, told Tracy she'd gotten everything she needed from her, and said, "Goodbye bitch!" Those were the last two words Tracy heard from Nicole.

I asked Tracy why this became a turning point in her decision to leave the gay lifestyle. I questioned her as to why she simply didn't look for another partner that could unconditionally love and appreciate her. Tracy told me that she had never been comfortable with the gay lifestyle because of her religious upbringing. As she reflected on this relationship and all the drama it had caused including almost losing her life, she thought about a statement that her mom had previously made. Tracy's mom told her she would come after her with a flashlight to save her from hell. This was eye-awakening for Tracy. Somehow these words left an impression of the seriousness of where Tracy would spend eternity and how close she had come to dying.

I challenged Tracy on the controversial nature of her belief that she had been healed from homosexuality. I explored with her the belief that many gay rights activists insist that homosexuality is something that you are born with, it is not a choice. I gave the example of how changing one's gender preference is often seen by some as the same as trying to change the color of one's skin— it is said that you simply can't do it.

When asked how she would respond to these objections, Tracy explained that for her it was a choice, she was not born that way. Her turning to women as lovers came out of pain and rejection from men starting with her father. Tracy said that her connection with women was an emotional connection, not a sexual one. She recalled times as a child that she had stepped in to protect her mother from abusive men. This defensive behavior continued in her relationship with Nicole. Tracy explained that she was attracted to women who were hurt by men and felt a need to protect them.

When I asked whether she ever felt tempted to go back when she saw attractive women, Tracy answered "yes", this was something she had to work on. Tracy explained that much like an ex-alcoholic, she saw herself as an ex-lesbian. She adamantly maintained however that God had delivered her from this lifestyle. Although she sees herself as being liberated from homosexuality, she is not without temptations to go back into that way of life. She relayed to me an incident in which she was supposed to hook up with a female at an airport. The potential prospect's plane was late which made it impossible to get together. Tracy saw this event as an answer to her prayers; an intervention by God.

She continually prays to God for help, wisdom, and discernment in overcoming what she describes as her "past lustful attraction to members of the same sex." For accountability Tracy feels that she can go to her pastor or his wife. Tracy explained she is an extremely private person and that there are not any support groups in her area. Her strongest anchor and support has been her faith in God.

I asked Tracy what good has come out of this experience. She told me that through this journey she has developed a strong, personal, and intimate relationship with God. In order to develop this bond, she made a decision to leave behind her lifestyle of drinking, partying, and having gay partners. Tracy explained that the same way an alcoholic has to stay away from bars and associating with friends that drink, she has to stay away from enablers and others that would entice her to go back into the gay lifestyle.

Because of this Tracy purposely does not attend gay parties anymore and is now dating heterosexual men. Although Tracy has chosen to be heterosexual, this does not preclude her from having gay platonic friends and supporting the rights of gays to have gay relationships. As of my last contact with Tracy, since our initial meeting approximately five years ago, she told me that life is good. Tracy continues to date men and has left the gay lifestyle behind. She told me that she is in a much better place emotionally and her faith in God continues to get her through any past feelings of hurt towards her dad, men, and any difficulties she encounters on a daily basis.

Chapter 2

Leila, the "No Good Girl"

Healed from Crack Cocaine, Rape, and Prostitution

Like Tracy (Chapter One), Leila was rejected at birth by her biological father. Unfortunately, she was also rejected by her mother. At the age of 3 months, as Leila laid neglected, half-dead, and bleeding from her navel, Leila's mother made a choice to give her away. In Leila's autobiographical vignette, *Still Standing* (2008), Leila states that her mom was in love with a man who said to her, "if you want me, then you need to get rid of the children." Strangely enough, Leila's cousin made her mother an offer that she could not refuse. He told Leila's mom that he would buy her a pair of shoes if she let him have Leila because his wife was barren. Leila's older sibling went to her biological aunt and her mother was allowed to keep her half sister who was fathered by her mother's boyfriend.

Leila describes in her book a life that followed her adoption of continuous parental neglect, physical and sexual abuse, crack cocaine addiction, and prostitution in a small rural town outside of Columbus, Georgia. Ironically, as we will come to learn, some of the poor choices Leila's biological mother made were repeated by Leila in her own life.

Following the unforeseen and premature death of her adoptive dad (her cousin), Leila at the age of 24 months old, was left without a strong, reliable, and loving paternal figure in the home. Consequently, she was unprotected and had to suffer and endure constant physical beatings from her adoptive mother who was an alcoholic suffering from depression. Frequently her adoptive mother would beat and threaten to kill her and tell Leila that no one would care if she died.

Among the many other abuses Leila suffered at the hands of her adoptive mother were a fractured spine, damaged eyelid, and rape at the age of seven by a 60 year old man who was the brother-in-law of her adoptive mother. On one occasion she was beat in the vagina with an extension cord because a cousin touched her while she was asleep alongside some other children in the back seat of a car. Her adoptive mother tied her hands while she beat her and told her this was to teach her a lesson. From then on, Leila learned to never go to sleep while her adoptive mother was awake because doing so meant that she would be beaten for almost any reason.

At the age of 12 following the death of her adoptive mother due to a heart attack she suffered, Leila went to live with her adoptive mother's sister. There the beatings continued and she was raped by three adoptive cousins, two of which were grown men. Leila did not report the rapes to anyone because of the past mishandling of rapes inflicted upon her. As a result, these cousins were never prosecuted.

After a short period of time, Leila went to live with her biological mother. This was not a respite however, because not only was she beaten by her mother's husband, but her mother was beaten by him as well. Leila found out later that her mother had reclaimed her because by doing so her mom received the monthly Social Security benefit check from Leila's deceased dad. Leila eventually ran away from this abusive home and took up residence with her older sister.

Regrettably, Leila did not fare any better at her sister's home. The pattern of abuse, beatings, and dysfunctional relationships continued. At the age of 16 Leila was homeless. After attempting suicide in the middle of a street intersection, she was rescued by an angel by the name of Elma Smith, who allowed Leila to live with her husband and two daughters. Like Laurie as you will read in Chapter Three, Leila experienced with this family her first sense of genuine love, caring, and healthy parenting. Tragically, the pattern of abuse was so deeply woven into Leila's spirit she could not take advantage of and remain long in this environment.

The damage to Leila's self-esteem and her sense of worthlessness was so profoundly ingrained in Leila's spirit that she eventually left this family and returned to the familiar life of abuse, dysfunction, and searching for love from man to man. According to Leila, she could no longer be a child, she had seen and been exposed to so much adult behavior and demonic activities that there was no turning back. The damage had been done.

After becoming pregnant at 16 from a married man who rejected her, Leila, still homeless, continued to go from man to man. On one occasion she attempted to kill the baby by taking a lot of pills, laxatives, and pain medications to abort it, but her son survived. When this did not work, Leila gave up and reasoned that God wanted her to have the baby.

She also feared that if she continued with these attempts to abort the baby, she might end up with a deformed or disabled infant.

Remarkably, Leila was able to finish high school even though she was transient and homeless. She did eventually marry her high school sweetheart, who she had a genuine loving relationship absent of any abuse, but the marriage did not last. He abandoned her because his mother interfered, adamantly opposed the marriage, and referred to Leila as the "no good girl." On paper however, the marriage lasted 15 years and they continued to see each other sporadically. Both joined the army, but he eventually left the service.

Leila's downward spiral happened after she went overseas and was separated from her husband, her true love. She descended into drinking and partying all night with men. Leila started using drugs and eventually had to use them to wake up, stay up, and go to sleep. After 10 years in the army she had to leave because of her non-stop drug use. Pills, Acid, Speed, LSD, and Hash had gotten the best of her.

Back in the States, Leila's descent continued as she ended up living with a man who was on the run from the law. Leila became pregnant with his child and both continued to evade the authorities. Their house was a base house and by then she was addicted to crack cocaine— selling and using it. To support her habit, she would sell her food stamps and body. Leila stole food and diapers for her two children and taught her oldest son how to help her steal food. Following the birth of her third child, Leila writes in her book that she gave this baby up for adoption and left the hospital to get crack, all in the same day.

Eventually, Leila landed up in prison and her oldest son was also handcuffed and taken away as well. It was in jail and through the various prison ministries that Leila was able to turn her life around. One night while she was in jail she had a dream in which God told her that he wanted her to take his word to the people. He said that her story of her own life would speak to them. In addition, Leila greatly benefitted from the court provided individual counseling she received from licensed therapist, Dr. Beverly Willis. She helped Leila to deal with her victim mentality and low self-esteem. It was also in jail at the age of 32 that Leila made a decision to leave the drugs behind so that she would never be separated from her children again. Leila quit cold turkey and has been free from drugs for 26 years.

However, Leila's path to recovery since her release from jail was not smooth sailing. Leila told me that even now she is still learning and growing. She has continued to have some rocky times due to damage that had been done during her early years and also in the lives of her own children. One consequence of Leila's rearing is that the cycle of abuse repeated itself in the life of her daughter. To Leila's regret, her daughter between the ages of six and eight was sexually abused by her second husband on an ongoing basis.

At that time he was a lay pastor at their same church and Leila doubted whether he in fact had abused her daughter. Leila tried to help both of them and allowed him to stay in their house which unfortunately prolonged the abuse of her daughter. Her pastor eventually persuaded Leila that her daughter was telling the truth. Leila, her son, and daughter subsequently confronted Leila's husband, who was then adjudicated and sent to prison.

Understandably, her current relationship with her daughter Jamila still has some rifts between them. In spite of the counseling her daughter received and an admittance that she has forgiven her mother, there are still obstacles in their relationship with one another. Leila's daughter did not take well to counseling and discontinued services after a short stint. She still has trust issues with men and smokes to relieve stress. Although a rift remains between Leila and her daughter, they are on speaking terms and continue to work on their relationship.

I asked Leila whether she thought the cycle of abuse had stopped with her daughter and whether her grandchildren are at risk and susceptible to abuse. According to Leila, the grandchildren are doing well and are properly cared for and supervised by their mother, fathers, grandparents, and herself.

Leila's eldest son, Roderick, met an untimely death at the age of 39 from a massive seizure. The autopsy revealed that he had stopped taking his seizure medication which doctors believed led to his death. Up until his demise, Roderick was her favorite child and they had a great relationship. Her youngest son, Derhonte is a musician and has created both secular and gospel CDs. He is the drummer at Leila's church and is gainfully employed as an Apple technician. Despite the challenges Derhonte encountered from growing up in a dysfunctional household, they have been able to work on their issues and now have a good relationship.

Leila has tried to reconnect with her next to the youngest son, Preston, (who she released for adoption at birth) when he turned 21. She was unsuccessful however, and was blocked by her limited finances, fear of rejection, and the concern that she did not have enough to offer him. Leila did try on another occasion to find him before he turned 21, but stopped herself because she didn't want to break up his home if he was happy with his adoptive parent(s). She still hopes to one day meet and reconnect with him.

Leila noted that after she gave her life to Christ she has had to make daily conscious choices to leave her enabling buddies, neighborhood, and lifestyle of drugs and prostitution behind her. Leila acknowledged that she has been able to triumph over her demons with the help of Dr. Willis and her current pastor, Bishop Ann Hardman who Leila has been with for over 20 years.

I caught up with Leila by telephone about five years after we had originally met at a Women's Empowerment speaking engagement. I questioned how her victimized childhood and life experiences had impacted her as a Christian, a woman, and what effect it had on her faith and relationship with God. I asked as I did Tracy, (Chapter One) what good has come out of this experience.

Leila told me that she does not blame God for the negative things that have happened to her. Instead she sees them as a part of God's plan for her life. Leila explained that the enemy tried to destroy her, but God's plan was that she would live and not die. According to Leila, he allowed her to go through this so that she could bring healing and deliverance to broken and hurting people.

Leila's passion now is to share and use her testimony of how she was healed by God so that others may be rescued and set free. Her goal is to enable others to free themselves from the clutches of dysfunctional parenting, addiction, rape, abuse, and poverty. She attributes God's grace and mercy as to why and how she was able to leave a torrid past behind that had her life and her offspring's marked for death and destruction.

As of this writing, Leila continues to allow herself to be used by God through her testimony of how she has overcome the horrendous abuses of those who were in positions of authority over her life. She continues to work in the church with her beloved pastor rescuing others from the streets as she herself had been rescued by her pastor. Leila uses her book, *Still Standing* when she speaks to serve as a mouthpiece and a call to action so that she can reach lost and abandoned souls.

Absent in Leila's demeanor and words are the depression, heart-ache, "why me?", and the frequent nursing and rehearsing of past victim-izations that many abused individuals hold on to. She is indeed an overcomer that loves life and people. Leila's outlook on life is positive, cheerful, and filled with optimism. In 2013, she married a university professor who is a practicing Christian. He has never been abusive towards her. Personally, she is a joy to be around; her words are inspiring and always filled with hope and love. Leila has forgiven her past abusers and has truly been healed by God!

Chapter 3

Laurie, "YOU STUPID PIECE OF SHIT!"

Healed from Parental Abuse, Incest, and Rape

Laurie, age 49, was born in Albuquerque, New Mexico to parents of Canadian descent. She has dual citizenship because her dad was stationed in the Canadian Service and traveled the Eastern Seaboard, back and forth between Canada and the United States. In her biography, radio interviews, and blog posts she describes the pain her entire family suffered due to what she deemed ignorance, a lack of education, and the cycle of abuse and poverty that repeated itself, having been passed from her grandparents to her parents. According to Laurie, her parents did not break the cycle but instead perpetuated it by inflicting Laurie and her siblings with continuous abuse which spanned over two decades.

The ensuing passage is an excerpt from Laurie Ann Smith's auto-biography, A *Life of Death: The Redemption* (2001). I thought it best for Laurie to share her story as only she can articulate it in her own words:

> 'Nooooooooooooooooooooooo!' I yelled as my knee came in contact with the inside of the hot oven door. I struggled, but it did no good. My knees were burning as my mom was pushing my hands onto the oven racks.
>
> 'AaaaaYYYYYYYYYYYYYY!!!!!!!!!'I screamed 'LOOK WHAT YOU ARE MAKING ME DO!!!!' she

yelled at me. 'I TOLD YOU TO STAY OUT OF MY WAY GOD DAMN YOU!!!! YOU ARE DOING THIS TO YOURSELF, YOU STUPID PIECE OF SHIT!!!' she screamed at me as she stood behind me and was literally shoving me into the oven

I remember being brought into the living room and beaten, all the while she was cursing me. As I stood there and cried, the palms of my hands burned and my knees were killing me. The burn on my side was what started the whole ordeal as I had come through the kitchen while my mom was pulling a sheet pan of cookies out of the oven.

It was summer time and I had a halter top on. As I walked by, she turned with the sheet pan and ran into my side with it. Instead of setting the pan down to see if I was okay she became angry and turned vicious, shouting at me and burning me.

'Noooooooooooooooooooooooooo!' I yelled. I was crying hysterically. Suddenly I woke up and realized it was just another one of my nightmares. I had them regularly and each one seemed worse than the one before.

I got up and went to jump in the shower. Throwing my sleep shirt on the floor I looked into the mirror, looking at the scar from that day in the 'house of hell' on Indian School Road.

It had faded some. I had received that lovely memoir from my mom when I was only 11-years old. The scar was nearly 20-years old now and was fading over time, but over time, but it was still quite big and noticeable.

I had often woke myself up crying out while dreaming about my mom's abusive behavior toward me. When Cecil and I moved to Edmonton I woke us both up quite often. I was crying and sobbing uncontrollably as he held me, listened to me and tried to console me.

My mom was right! She had warned me that she would 'haunt' me until the day I died and so far she had been accurate. I turned the shower on and pulled the shower curtain back as I looked in the mirror at my back and the damaged blood vessels that left a dark shadow on a protruding lump on the right side of my spine near my neck.

I had hardly no feeling there anymore. The nerves had been damaged from being beaten with the rolling pin and slammed and tossed into walls. Most days I wouldn't even think about the scars and deep tissue damage done those many years be fore, but after the recent reoccurring dreams of the abuse my mom inflicted upon me, it left me feeling angry and all the hatred would come rushing back.

I could hear her voice as she verbally abused me. Now she was gone and I had no way to ever reconcile with her. I had no way to ask her to apologize for what she had done to me and to all of us for that matter. I wanted her to tell me she actually did want me, and that I was her special girl and that she did not mean to hurt me. I wanted to hear all of that from her lips, from her mouth, but now all I had were bad dreams, fading scars and a desire to scream my head off. That first year in Calgary was a long one and I focused on work and trying to stay sane. (138; ch. 21)

Laurie's story was not easy to believe or digest. When I first read this excerpt in Laurie's blog, I assumed it was a bad dream, a nightmare she was recalling. I saw the picture she posted of herself as the young seven year old girl that had been so badly abused by her parents. She had a face any mother or dad would love— light freckles, blue eyes, and wispy blond hair separated into two ponytails. Her demeanor was quiet, appealing, and soft spoken.

Surely, this could not be true I told myself, this could not have happened in the United States; home of the free, land of the brave. Weren't their laws to protect children? What about brave neighbors, teachers, and other adults that would boldly stand up and intervene on behalf of an abused child? My thoughts wrestled within as I tried to deny the undeniable. I questioned how this was allowed to happen. I asked myself how a parent could be so cruel. Curious about its veracity, I contacted and interviewed Laurie on my talk show, *Inspirational Voices* to get some much needed answers. Sadly, Laurie's story checked out; she had the scars and many stories behind them to prove their authenticity.

Laurie's story of incest, rape, sodomy, and the resulting aftermath of infertility disturbed me as well. I've often wondered why I couldn't just click the mouse and turn to another page, but I was hooked as I read and listened to her account of the ordeal which began at the age of eight.

Call it compassion, empathy; I've always had a hard time turning away from someone in pain, especially children. After reading her account of how she overcame her traumatic past and reading her mission statement, "To stop child abuse and all forms of human rights abuses," I knew instantly that her story of *Redemption* had to be included in this anthology. I could not turn away and hope someone else would help support her cause, I felt obligated to do my part.

Again, I will share in Laurie's own words her account of the incest, sodomy, and rape she suffered as a child:

> 'How much will you give me for it?' I asked. 'The most I can do is one fifty,' the pawn dealer said as he carefully checked out the amp and guitar. 'Is that the best you can do?' I was hoping for twice that amount. 'Yes, take it or leave it, that's all I'm giving for these,' he said very professionally.
>
> He knew he had me over a barrel and I desperately needed the money. 'Alright...' I said giving in to his offer. I then proceeded to take the money, left the pawn shop, jumped in my car and drove home.
>
> No one was there except my cat, Zeus. He had been with me since we lived on La Veta Street. We had moved away from the block almost two years before to the southeast part of the city—'gang land' as I call it. Gangs walked around swinging chains, bats, and weapons. Mattresses and other debris would be set on fire almost daily and left burning in the street.

Store clerks were held up at gunpoint on a regular basis. It was not a pleasant condition and was extremely dangerous.

My friend Mike had been held up at gunpoint three times in the past 3-weeks in a convenience store two blocks from me where he worked part-time. I wasn't scared as I had grown up with my life being threatened by two of the biggest monsters I could think of. They were harmless now, though, being too old and too mellowed out to get overly abusive about anything; although my mother still loved to get her digs in when possible. They were at my brothers funeral in Canada.

My sister was due in January and it was already October. She was six months pregnant, but she still went to the funeral with my parents. I did not go as it was decided that I should stay and look after the cat, and also the fact that no one had any money for travel expenses.

I did not have a dime to my name and had to pawn my amp and guitar just to pay for my car insurance that month. My days of partying were just about over as I thought about my brother and how he had ended his life so abruptly. Rob was a coke head and had been for years. He was often homeless and could not keep a regular job for very long. Howard was the same way, although he was just a pill popper, but homeless on the streets of Calgary just the same.

Rob had tried to kill himself many times before. On one occasion he almost succeeded, but made the mistake of calling us from Canada. He had slit his wrists and was bleeding to death, but decided to phone my mom. She got him to tell her where he was at the time as he was homeless and had been using drugs for years. She put me on the phone with him and I talked to him while she went across the street to a neighbors to use their phone.

She then called our oldest brother, Kevin, who was living in Calgary and told him the information. Kevin then phoned the ambulance and brother was saved just in time. While I had been talking on the phone to my dying brother, he said some very strange things to me, but I thought it was because he was high or because he was hallucinating from losing all the blood he had already lost.

He said to me, whispering into the phone, 'Your skin was so soft, so soft, and smooth.' I was just going along with it as I had talked to Rob and Howard when they were on drugs before and knew the scenario very well. We used to sit in the back yard and discuss politics, the government and our crazy parents for hours when they were high. I used to have to talk my brother out of robbing stores, blowing peoples homes up, stabbing my sister and these types of crazy things. I should have gone into the Police Force Special Teams Unit to talk people out of these types of situations because I definitely had the experience needed.

I was twelve-years old the last time I had seen Rob as he had went back to Canada and did not return to visit us.

'Your skin was so smooth,' he whispered, 'not in a baby smooth way, but a sexual way,' he said to me. I was suprised to hear him say that to me as I had fully blocked out that memory of someone molesting me when I was a young girl— until now.

I thought it had been my dad, and wanted to blame my dad for it, but as I grew older each year it seemed more likely that my brother was the one who molested me. I used to sleep with my blankets wrapped tightly around my body like a mummy for years after and as a young adult I did not like anyone touching me.

One time in junior high a young guy came up to me and (as a sad, but silly joke) grabbed my crotch and then took off. It was the thing guys were doing in those days. I got so upset that I chased him down and kicked him in the balls as hard as I could. Then when he fell down to the ground in pain, I beat the crap out of him. My shop teacher saw what happened and ran over to break it up and calm me down. I do not remember the boy's name, but he apologized to me and stayed clear of me for the rest of his life.

What I do remember about the sexual abuse I suffered is fragmented and not very clear as I had blocked it out for many years. I can remember biting either his nose or his ear as hard as I could and was punched in the face because of it. I know that I wanted to believe it was my dad because I hated my dad already and I loved my brother, Rob. I hated my dad for what he did to my mother, to our brothers, to our family, and the lack of real fatherly love and care he had shown for all those years.

I would eventually come to realize, many years later, that he did not have the skills or the ability to be a father. And, even to this day, does not understand the pain he put his family through. My dad talks about the 'good old days' with a gleam in his eye, and when he mentions his youth it was always the best. They were poor, but they had a great life he says.

I heard other stories about his parents that are quite conflicting, so my dad and I do not talk about his past or our family's past to this day. My mom told me years ago that, when she was growing up, she was beat on and whipped on a regular basis. Her mother was very abusive towards her, her husband and all their children.

My grandmother horsewhipped my uncle, forced him to sleep in the bitter cold and he died. She apparently had no remorse. She horsewhipped my mother for no reason, too, and who knows what else she did to her children.

My grandmother took in a bunch of orphans from an orphanage that was overcrowded back in the 1930's. My mom was born in 1927, my dad 1923...during the Great Depression Era.... My grandmother had taken these orphans in to help on the farm, but most of them ran away and took their chances on the road due to my grandmother beating and whipping them like dogs, my mother said.

> My mom and my grandmother did not speak for many years. I met my grandmother when she came to visit when I was 12-years old and I did not like her at all. Even to this day I cannot bring my heart to like or accept her. She was the only grandparent I got to meet as the rest had all passed on either before I was born or shortly after. It was all passed on from generation to generation, this horrible disease called 'hatred....'
>
> My entire life consisted of hatred, anger, sadness and despair. I thought about the way my mom had treated me. She did not treat my sister, Kathi, that way. She had only slapped Kathi around a little, but I never saw her beating on her with a belt, a table leg, a rolling pen, or her fists. She truly loved Kathi and I feel it was because Kathi was not born out of marital rape, as I was.
>
> My mom just could not deal with having to see me as she hated the very act that produced me. Every time she looked at me was a brutal reminder of the abuse she suffered (and the abuse I would eventually suffer from because of it). (102; ch. 16)

As gripping and incredulous as Laurie's story was, I found out that the reason I couldn't just click the mouse and turn to another page was because of her ending! Often when we hear of, or see painful images we want to immediately turn away because we feel helpless and hopeless. But, like a well written mystery that keeps you in suspense until the ending, I learned that her finale was a victorious one that offered hope and healing for the many worldwide sufferers of abuse in its diverse forms. I was compelled to read on and learn more about her victory over an egregious childhood.

In my interview with Laurie I was even more overwhelmed with her tenacity, her ability to endure, and the remarkable capacity of the human spirit to go through a fiery furnace and come out without the stench of smoke from their afflictions. I had to include her story, especially the ending which highlighted the redemptive steps she took towards healing and wholeness. I had to share it in order to let individuals who are suffering from any form of abuse know that there is hope, and as Laurie explains in her blog posts and writings— redemption.

Laurie shared with me that at the age of 21 she confronted the generational demons that had plagued her entire family. Laurie explained that after nine years of involving herself in drugs and a partying lifestyle to escape the abuse and self-loathing, she came face to face with the enemy within herself.

Laurie attributed this epiphany to four major life altering events. The first occurred when she made a decision to stay off drugs and live. This revelation came to her following the tragic death of one of her older brothers who was a cocaine addict who committed suicide the year before. This event jolted her into the reality that she was going down the same road her brother had traveled and she too was headed for a fatal collision if she did not stop using drugs. The second event she attributed this metamorphosis to was being born again on May 22, 2007. Laurie told me that God has really been a "healer in her life." She described herself as not knowing how lost she was. After receiving the Lord Jesus Christ as her personal Lord and Savior, she "was able to truly heal by the precious healing Word of our Lord."

Although Laurie has never received any type of traditional counseling, she stated that online blogging was the third event that helped her to vent, understand, and work through the trauma of her upbringing. Blogging helped her to see that her voice did count, and that by publically blogging her experiences she felt that she was no longer trapped in the silence and shame of being a victim of domestic violence.

Laurie chose to form a union with other bloggers who have received counseling or who were working through their issues of PTSD (post traumatic stress disorder), DID (dissociative identity disorder), and other issues caused or compounded by trauma. According to Laurie, this unification helped her to move from being a victim to a "survivor."

Laurie recalled that by the time she became a teenager, she had seen so much destruction she simply copied and mirrored what she knew— violence, hatred, abuse, and destruction. Laurie thought that her life would continue along this path of devastation since her "family had… already been destroyed by poverty, hatred, marital abuse, child abuse, drug abuse that went on and on without end."

According to Laurie, reflecting on the memories of Deserie Loges' family that took her in and provided a respite from the fury and madness at La Veta Street was the fourth event that was instrumental in her transformation. Like Leila, (Chapter Two) this family showed Laurie that she should not hate others or herself. By modeling love and allowing

Laurie to bond with their family, Laurie gradually learn to love, believe in, and prove to herself that she was worthy of a good life.

Laurie realized through this bonding experience that all things were possible. Knowingly or unknowingly, this family had planted a seed in Laurie while she was young and at the right time it blossomed which allowed her to reverse the negative curse her parents had instilled in her. Laurie meekly stated that to this family she owes her love and gratitude, and to God her very existence.

Laurie wholeheartedly believes that she has broken the generational curse of abuse because she has learned to not hurt herself or others. It is said that hurting people, hurt others. Interestingly, Laurie had to first learn to love herself before she was she able to shake off the negative images and messages that her parents infused in her. Currently, Laurie does not have any children due to infertility which resulted from the incest, rape, and sodomy, but she believes that if she had children, she would not abuse them.

Today, Laurie is a contributing writer for Northern Books, a new project co-founded with her long time friend and author Donna M. Kshir. Laurie is also a self-published author who has used her own funds to pay for all of her books. She continues to blog online frequently on her Blog Talk radio show. In addition, Laurie is also working on finishing a Bachelor's degree in Ministry and then hopes to go on to get a Master's degree in Biblical Studies, Old and New Testament. Following the completion of these degrees, she plans to get a Doctorate of Theology in Pauline Studies.

After graduation, she plans to continue writing in hopes "to honor and glorify our Lord Jesus Christ and be ready to serve the Lord in whatever capacity He wills." According to Laurie, her aim in telling her story is not to seek revenge. She too, like the others in this anthology, has forgiven her abusers. Her hope is that as people read her books, listen to her speeches, or talk with her online, they will see that survivors of child abuse, or any kind of abuse, "need to keep reaching out, keep their hope alive, and keep moving forward in their journey to have the life they deserve to have."

Chapter 4

Natalie, the "Perfect College Preppy"

Healed from Sexual Promiscuity

It is said that no one knows what happens behind closed doors. This adage definitely rang true in Natalie's life. It's ironic, that Natalie, "a daddy's girl" and a "PK" (Preacher's Kid) would make the claim that she was healed from sexual promiscuity which originated from paternal abandonment. It would be the last thing one would expect given that she was the long awaited fulfillment of her parents' wishes to finally have a baby girl. To their surprise and amazement, she was born 15 years after the birth of her next to the oldest brother.

Natalie was born into a well educated family on the west side of town in Joliet, Illinois to a *Father Knows Best* family. Natalie's dad was an extremely intelligent man who became the first African-American Civil Engineer in his region. He was well respected in the community not only because of his educational accomplishments, but because he was a preacher. Natalie's mom did not have to work and could have stayed home and played the suburban housewife, but she liked working as a CNA (Certified Nurse Assistant), and did so for over 30 years. Natalie's two older brothers are college graduates and both now hold prestigious job positions.

Unfortunately, the chaos that ensued from this idyllic family revolved around her dad's diagnosis of bipolar disorder and the death of close family members. Natalie's dad's mental condition when controlled by meds kept the family's homeostasis intact for the most part. However, when not on the meds, he experienced extreme paranoia, restlessness, insomnia, and panic attacks. This caused their relationship to deteriorate from the close father/daughter relationship wherein he taught her to ride a bicycle and they would watch movies together, to one episode in particular in which he threw her on the bed, called her abusive names, and locked her in the house.

The second misfortune was the multiple deaths of her paternal grandparents and paternal uncle when Natalie was 11 years old. This series of deaths in close succession caused her dad to quickly spiral downhill which resulted in a total upheaval of their *Father Knows Best* family. To this day her memories are few and far between when it comes to remembering a time when she had a pleasant time with him.

What Natalie remembers is the physical presence of her dad in the home, but absent were emotional feelings of love, closeness, and protection. Gone as well were her hopes of a mentally stable dad she could talk to. She also feared her dad would not be able to walk her down the aisle and give his approval to a prospective husband.

Natalie's brothers told her that she never knew her real father. According to Natalie in her autobiography, *From The Chaos To The Call*:

> Before his breakdown, he was a man always willing to help others in need. My father, mother and brothers would go on

> family vacations all the time and they had tons of fun together....Thinking back, I had a lot of restless nights as a child. I would have nightmares. It was almost like I sensed something wasn't right, but I couldn't put my finger on it (25).

Natalie further explains in her book that, "The feeling of safety had gone down the drain, after the countless number of his manic episodes" (27-28). In addition, she details how his illness influenced their father-daughter and other relationships with males, family members, and close friends. In *From The Chaos To The Call*, she takes the reader on a journey through her puberty, adolescence, and college years detailing how she coped with her dad's illness using the drug of sexual promiscuity.

Natalie clearly shows the reader in her book how the emotional absence, rejection, and yearning for a father to positively affirm her, drove her to use sex with men to meet those needs. For instance, while in nursing school and knowing the risks of contracting HIV/AIDS, against her better judgment she chose at times to have unprotected sex. Natalie faulted these and other poor decisions on the enemy (Satan) at work in her life attempting to thwart the plan that God had for it.

Individuals without a strong religious background as Natalie, (she was a PK and attended church about four times a week) may not agree that the enemy was at work, but simply adolescent rebellion, immaturity, low self-esteem, and poor judgment in response to her dad's illness. Regardless of how one chooses to define or interpret Natalie's handling of her dad's illness, it is clear by the end of her story that her past life of sexual promiscuity, use of profanity, and immaturity are well behind her.

What I want to examine and focus on now however, as I did with all the other overcomers in this anthology, is how Natalie was able to make a major transformation of her thoughts, actions, and governing principles. I did not have to ask or dig deeply to discover Natalie's epiphany. Fortunately, she had carefully and skillfully laid out the path and principles she used in her book to obtain deliverance from a life of sexual promiscuity. Most importantly, she explains how the reader can also apply the word of God to bring restoration in their own lives from this addiction.

Natalie prefaced that in order to be healed, she first had to acknowledge and accept that her low self-esteem was a heart condition. Natalie, hurt by her father, healed by God, explained that her healing came by reasoning that, "since it is on the inside, only the Creator can deliver you from it." She clarified by saying that "only God knew what was really going on with me, even when I didn't know myself" (39). Natalie described in her book the steps she took were as follows:

1. Separate from people who are connected to your bondage.
2. Surround yourself with Godly friends and mentors.
3. Get to know your Father (Heavenly) (97-101)

These steps led Natalie to her purpose, which is to reach back and minister to every young woman who is experiencing the pain of not having a stable dad and to speak positive words into their lives.

As of this writing, some seven years later, Natalie has matured in her interpersonal relationships. Gone are the days of going from man to man to seek affirmation and acceptance. She has been married to her loving and supportive husband, Michael Deon Flemons for 14 years. And, yes, by the grace of God, Natalie's dad gave his approval and walked her down the aisle.

Natalie describes her relationship with her husband as an example of God's love and faithfulness. Remarkably, she and her husband have recently become ordained ministers. They gladly share their home with Natalie's mom and enjoy her love and companionship. This allows Natalie to watch over her mom as she declines in age. In addition to Natalie now having an intact home and emotional life, she is also fulfilled as well in her career as a Registered Nurse.

In thought, mind, and actions, Natalie is a new creature. The old ways are passed away. She is now a Christian believer based on her own testimony of God's goodness in her life versus her parents' witness or belief system. Today, Natalie shares her testimony of hope and encouragement as an evangelist to women and whomever God sends her to. She is also the CEO/Founder of *Fertilizing Your Faith*, a ministry for couples dealing with the challenges of infertility. Natalie can be contacted through Facebook at *Author Natalie C. Flemons* or by email at chaos2call@yahoo.com.

Chapter 5

Teri, the "Spawn of Satan"

Healed from Misogyny and Abusive Pastors

Teresa Myers is the author of *Persecuted Saints Within the Church Walls* (2008), an autobiography in which she details abuses encountered at the hands of church pastors, leaders, and members of a non-denominational church. Teresa, affectionately known as *"Teri",* details within her book her account of trying to find a niche in the church community. Teri's hope to use her God given gifts and talents was initially well received, but later was met with disappointment, accusations, abandonment, misuse, and eventually ex-communication from the church.

Teri's spirituality and beliefs have been influenced by at least three generations of family members. As a child she was taught the serenity prayer by her great grandmother, Helen Gillespie. She recalled fondly how her great grandmother always encouraged and prayed for her. Not only did she dote on Teri, but her great grandmother had a heart for hurting people and they would often stop her even at a shopping mall and ask her to pray for them. Teri's great grandfather taught her spiritual things pertaining to the word of God. Her grandfather on the other hand, Edward, did deliverance services in their home with the aim of purging out the demonic side of individuals.

Although Teri's parents were believers, they had an acrimonious relationship which resulted in a dysfunctional and unpleasant home life. Visits to her great grandparents' home provided a relief from the constant fighting between her parents. Teri's great grandmother was Protestant and her great grandfather was Catholic. Both were spirit filled believers. In the 50's, Teri's great grandmother converted to Catholicism.

During her childhood, a local Baptist Church sent a bus to her neighborhood to evangelize residents. At one church service, the pastor had an altar call when Teri was 13. He prayed and she accepted God into her life. At age 15, Teri like many troubled adolescents was caught up in her own personal insecurities. Coupled with these intense feelings, she lacked parental support because they were constantly fighting and unavailable to Teri emotionally or spiritually. It was during this chaotic period that she asked God to reveal himself to her or she would walk away from her relationship with Him. One Sunday morning, God did answer Teri's prayers during an altar call initiated by her pastor.

Teri's great grandmother, her rock and anchor, died when Teri was 21 years old. Before dying Teri asked God for her great grandmother's anointing of softness and gentleness. Teri described her great grandmother as a strong woman who loved people and was called a true servant. To Teri, her great grandparents were more like surrogate parents than great grandparents. Today, that gentleness and softness that Teri asked for is now evident in her large blue eyes and soft, but steadfast demeanor.

Teri's first marriage was at the age of 19. From this marriage her oldest daughter Tera was born. Teri described her ex-husband as a con artist who pretended to be a Christian. That marriage lasted three years. In retrospect, Teri explained that this marriage was simply a way for her to get out of the house and away from a dysfunctional lifestyle.

She has been married to her current husband, Bob Myers, for over 30 years. He legally adopted her three children and they jointly parented their youngest son. Bob has been a tremendous source of strength, love, and support to Teri and their children. The church also has given her the strength and encouragement she needed to make it through any difficult times. In searching for churches, Bob and Teri have always looked for a church that could also minister to their children.

Following a move to Florida, from Oklahoma, they decided to fellowship with Teri's aunt who was a member of an intercessory prayer group led by a preacher, who Teri facetiously nicknamed, "Apostle Odious." After visiting several times, she asked for prayer during a church service for a periodontal condition. As other believers gathered around her in prayer, Pastor Odious unabashedly asked whether she participated in oral sex with her husband. After a resounding, "No!" from Teri, Pastor Odious declared in the presence of others that her periodontal disease was the end result of the sin she was committing.

Teri continued, "At that point I looked at my aunt and told her that he was wrong in his assumption of me. With a pat on my back, my aunt told me that God was doing a work and for me to sit there, not saying anything, and accept it" (46). Needless to say, Teri and Bob were soon searching for a new body of Christian believers.

They subsequently relocated to Apopka, Florida. It was there that their then 17 year old daughter found a church that she loved and was totally ecstatic about it. Her siblings, Teri, and Bob got on the bandwagon and were just as much enthused and involved in the church as their kids. They were so moved and well received by this church that they chose to join and make it their church home. Teri and Bob ushered, Teri joined the Prayer Team, and they helped with painting, fundraising, and hosting youth events at their home. Teri went as far as donating her emerald and diamond ring to help with the new construction project.

Teri's prophetic gift started to grow in her late 20s, after lying dormant since her teens and early 20s. According to Teri, God gave her the gift of prophecy and visions. Initially, Teri was even encouraged by the pastor to use her gift of prophecy to give revelations to different church members. As the church grew, lives were saved and people were healed.

However, things suddenly changed after Teri returned from an Indiana visit to her family where she had ministered. Teri unsuspecting of any change was anxious to share with the church body the miracles God had performed through her in Indiana. An event that started the descent from the pastor's and members' graces occurred after she prayed for a couple that shared with other members how they had been slain in the spirit and blessed tremendously through Teri's prayers. The pastors became suspicious and for several months she was watched and members were asked to divulge the nature of their communications with her.

As time passed and Teri continued to experience success from her answered prayers, the senior pastor saw her as a threat and the parishioners complained about Teri. One family left the congregation and blamed her for their departure. The senior pastor told Teri that she was not called to be a prophet and she should take down any references to prophesying contained on her website. Things quickly began to spiral downhill after that reprimand. One evening the pastor called and asked for a face-to-face meeting at the church with Teri and her husband, Bob. Once there, they were joined by five other pastors of the church. The senior pastor yelled at Teri, told her that her prophecies were from Satan, and they were excommunicated.

The descent to hell as Teri described it began for the entire family. They were made to feel like "the spawn of Satan" according to her. Bob supported Teri through this ordeal, but was angry with God that he allowed this to happen. Although Teri and Bob could better handle the ex-communication, their children were hurt and devastated by it. They could no longer play with their friends in this small community. At the mall, church members walked the other way when they saw Teri's kids.

I asked Teri in a recent interview I conducted with her, how she came to grips with this experience as well as others detailed in her autobiography which some would see as faith shattering. I questioned how it impacted her as a Christian, a woman, and what effect it had on her faith in and relationship with God.

Teri professed that her faith in God is uncompromised and has grown stronger through these "persecutions." She reiterated the words in her book's introduction that, "many people might consider her book and the contents in it an attack against churches, pastors, and members." However, she explained that *Persecuted Saints Within the Church Walls* "is to help believers realize they have been holding on to a fantasy of a 'Perfect Church' where everyone gets along and is in harmony continuously without fail" (13-14). Teri cautioned that Christians should not blindly follow pastors, those in authority, or fellow believers, realizing that they are mortals and therefore capable of sinning and misleading the flock.

She further explained that out of her persecutions came her autobiography to serve as a warning to believers that they are responsible for developing a personal relationship with God. She sees her book as a compass to show Christians that if they spend time in prayer and fasting, God will speak to, guide, and give them gifts and talents that can be used to improve their lives and other individuals; both believers and non-believers.

In regards to being a woman, she noted that in Galatians 3, it clearly states that there should not be any discrimination between males and females in God's church. Consequently, she clarified that women should not be confined to doing "women's groups," but should assume all roles in the church according to the gifts and talents God has instilled within them.

Today, years later, Teri's love for Christ is undeniable. Because she has forgiven her abusers, she is not locked into the past nor has she turned her back on the church in any form or fashion. She may have been hurt by some church members, but she definitely has been healed by God. Teri is strong, courageous, and committed to do God's work wherever he leads her. Teri's passion is to spread the "good news" and to set at liberty the bruised and broken-hearted within and outside the church walls. Her desire is for the church to display the unconditional love that God tells us we must have for one another.

Teri's love for the church, the pastors, and its members, prompts her to continue to fast, pray for and support them; they are proudly her family, and have made her who she is. Her position is clear— find a Bible-based church, support the body of Christ, but most importantly, develop a personal relationship with God so that He can lead, guide, and give you wisdom and spiritual discernment as you journey through life.

Chapter 6

Pastor Donnie, the "Homosexual Addict"

Healed from Rape and Homosexuality

It is often said that it rains on the just and on the unjust. It was no different for well-known Grammy, award-winning, and national recording artist, Donnie McClurkin. He too, has had his share of torrential rains in his life. Another adage often quoted in explaining universal truths is that the deeper the foundation, the taller the building will be. At 6'1" this holds true for Donnie's physical stature. In the world at large he stands tall as well having earned credits and awards as an American gospel singer and minister. He has won three Grammy awards, ten Stellar awards, two BET awards, two Soul Train awards, one Dove award and one NAACP Image award. He is one of the top selling Gospel music artists, selling over 10 million albums worldwide.

Donnie's autobiographical story is told in his book, *Eternal Victim, Eternal Victor* (2001). In it Donnie describes the love and redemption he found growing up in a dysfunctional home with nine siblings and "two parents that didn't have the issues of their own past resolved and healed [who] fought their wars in front of their children, with the children caught in the middle." Donnie states in his book that he was "born and raised in a sea of women, and didn't know how to adequately interact with men." Although his dad at times was physically in the home, he drank heavily and was described by Donnie as a "weekend alcoholic." Both parents were combative, violent, and abusive towards each other.

Growing up his family history and familial relationships were convoluted and twisted and interspersed with deception. Donnie unravels them and explains the family tree and interactions in his autobiography. His mother, Frances, was a product of incest and rape. She was fathered by her grandmother's husband and raised by her grandmother, who was affectionately called, "Mumma." Frances, his mother, was confused about her biological parents until the age of sixteen when it was revealed to her that the woman she referred to as sister (Donnie's biological maternal grandmother) was in fact her biological mother who had been raped by Mumma's husband.

Donnie's dad, Donald Sr., was born and raised in South Carolina. He was one of eight children. His father, (Donnie's paternal grandfather), John McClurkin, was a college taught Baptist pastor of two churches and his mother, Emma (Donnie's paternal grandmother), was the typical southern, submissive housewife. She cared for the children, grandchildren, and any illegitimate children born to young unmarried relatives that wanted a second chance in life.

On top of this precarious and "unstable" foundation, at the age of eight Donnie's life began its downward spiral. At the time, his parents' relationship was a tumultuous one and they were already separated and living apart. During this period Donnie was left to care for his two year old brother, Thomas, in an ungated yard while his mother was in the house. Donnie, a child himself at the age of eight and in need of supervision, was given the responsibility to watch over his two year old brother. As Donnie ran to retrieve a ball in the street, unbeknownst to him, his baby brother followed him and was struck and killed by a car. Sadly, his parents held Donnie responsible and he was left feeling unloved and with the emotional burden, rebuff, and guilt that he had killed his baby brother.

Following the funeral his distraught parents left the children in the care of his Uncle Clarence. Donnie explains in his book that his parents did not know that this family member was a pedophile. That same night under his Uncle's care, Donnie was sexually abused and raped by him. According to Donnie this was the man that scarred him for life and was responsible for his downward descent into confusion, homosexuality, and low self-esteem.

At the age of 13, Donnie was again raped by this same uncle's son, Clarence Jr. However, Donnie was not the only family member affected by the death of his brother Thomas. In different ways, all members were devastated by his death. Reportedly, two of his sisters experienced and battled with issues of substance abuse.

Donnie explains that:

> A seed had been planted… A seed of homosexuality that would be my lot to struggle with for many years to come…. I was not born with these sexual tendencies. It had nothing to do with some false theory of genetic make-up. It wasn't

chromosomal, and had-nor has it in today's society, either-nothing to do with my DNA (34).

Like Tracy (Chapter One), he maintains that homosexuality was a choice as a result of acts imposed on him as a confused, traumatized, and molested child.

Donnie explains that the impact of this trauma:

> ...was the beginning of what would be a hard life ahead for me. For years, no...decades, I had to deal with issues that scared and scarred me, deeply... At 8 years old, I was hurled into a chasm of confusion by this violation of rape. This 'Pandora's Box' was opened in my pre-pubescence, and introduced me to adult sexuality, issues and perversion far beyond my years and definitely beyond my ability to escape without damage (33-34).

Donnie's healing was hampered and delayed because according to him:

> There were brothers [inside the church] who seemingly befriended me under the guise of mentorship, only to reveal their desire and purpose to further the perversion and increase the confusion....Singing on Sundays, after weekend rendezvous was commonplace. Seeing other 'Christians' in compromising places, yet faithfully, hypocritically, and deceptively at their posts in church as though nothing was wrong was typical (39).

Included in this pool of predators according to Donnie were a plethora of "UNHEALED ministers, gospel singers, musicians, pastors, bishops, and those in leadership" (40).

Donnie reveals in his book that his healing eventually came from his faith in God, reading and receiving revelations and understanding through the scriptures. At the age of nine he received and accepted Jesus as his personal savior. Even though Donnie had received Jesus, he states that his struggle was just starting. According to Donnie:

> Now, childhood games started to take on a different slant and rough housing with friends became a little more than adolescent 'rites-of-passage' into manhood. There were feelings and thoughts involved that I knew weren't right. There were compelling desires that made it really difficult to interact with my male best friends, or any males, at all. Attractions started to develop that were seemingly beyond my control at that age (35).

In spite of the sexual predators inside the church, Donnie still found solace in going— singing, listening to hymns, playing the piano, and reading and listening to the Word of God. He eventually found peace there. Although Donnie experienced a respite from the thoughts and sexual urges that troubled him, he states that his healing did not come until he forgave his abusers and accepted responsibility for the actions and changes he made since becoming an adult.

According to Donnie as an adult, he had to consciously counter the dysfunctional thoughts that turned into desires, and from desires to actions. Donnie does not claim responsibility for what happened to him as a child, but explained as an adult he is responsible if he continues to perpetuate these habitual acts on others. In his book he described it as a "full-blown addiction" that he had to break. An addiction that he stated was in his mind daily. These "lusts, sins, addictions, and inordinate passions" caused him to be separated from his "God-ordained purpose and effectiveness" (111).

Donnie does not lay out a seven or ten step program that he used to overcome what he calls his "addiction to homosexuality." Laced throughout his book, are Biblical scriptures with explanations as to how he applied them to forgiving his abusers, himself, and ridding himself of what he describes as addictive homosexual thoughts. Donnie explains this process of redemption as a deliberate prayer process that took years to overcome. Simply stating that he wanted to change was not enough. Donnie describes it as a process that required transparency, openness, forgiveness, and drawing near to God through prayer and fasting.

Personally, as a Christian believer I get and understand it. His testament of God's power to deliver and redeem is amazing as it is in the lives of all the other heroes and sheroes in this collection. But as a trained psychotherapist I was left with many questions. I reached out to Donnie twice via U.S. Mail to ask some questions that were not answered in his book concerning clarity on when and how he chose to end his homosexual behavior and the healing that took place with his abusers, but I did not receive a response.

The reasons for my questions have to do with his claim of being healed like Tracy (Chapter One) from homosexuality. Logic would dictate that if his assertion is accurate, then given the same application of the principles he used, this healing should be reproducible in the lives of others. Therefore, those who *want to be delivered* from homosexuality should be able to leave this lifestyle behind them with the application of the same principles that Donnie used. In other words, if Donnie's transformation is genuine, than it stands to reason that others who are in bondage to homosexuality and *want to be healed, can be.*

As I did with the other respondents in this book, I wanted to give Donnie's story the litmus test. In light of the recent Supreme Court ruling on same sex marriage, I felt many readers would want in-depth answers about the how and why of his transformation. It is clear in his book that he was hurt by those in authority over him, but how was he healed by God? What were the steps he took to become healed?

Unfortunately I was not able to converse with him. Consequently, my sharing of his story in this anthology is based on Donnie's book and his interview with Kirk Franklin on the website, *EmpoweringEverydayWomen.Com*. Therefore, I have extensively quoted from his book in order to maintain and preserve the integrity of his text and his story. It is written to let others know that there is redemption and healing in Jesus for those who desire to be changed.

As of the writing of this book, Donnie is reportedly heterosexual and has a twelve year old son who lives with his mother and step-father. According to an interview on TBN with Kirk Franklin, Donnie is making a concerted effort to jointly parent his son and to cover him so that the abuse Donnie experienced is not repeated in his son's life.

Again like Tracy (Chapter One), Donnie states in his book that good has come out of his past abuses. He too, through his valley experiences has developed a strong, personal, and intimate relationship with God. Also, like Tracy, in order to develop this closeness, he made a decision to "consciously counter the dysfunctional thoughts that turned into desires, and from desires to actions" (110-111). According to Donnie, these "lusts, sins, addictions, and inordinate passions" caused him to be separated from his "God-ordained purpose and effectiveness" (111).

Although Donnie has fame that he could use to his advantage, and is widely esteemed, he does not want to be seen as a crusader who delivers individuals from the homosexual lifestyle. He simply asserts in his book that he shares his story for those who "are not happy in this lifestyle and with these desires, and they want to be delivered and freed from it" (45). What he does want to be known for however, is that his message is "clear, as real today as the day he committed his life to Christ at nine years old." He states in his book as follows, "I want to introduce Jesus Christ to the world, not as a religious leader, but as an intimate friend who wants to radically change our lives." Donnie further explains, "I want the world to know that we can sit down and embrace Him, He can embrace us, and He can handle any problem we are going through. He loves each of us individually, one by one" (179).

Chapter 7

Rose, the "Jesus Killer"

Healed from Anti-Semitism and Genocide

Rose's story of redemption through Jesus Christ is featured online at the website Jewishvoice.org (99). Like Tracy and Donnie in preceding chapters, Ms. Price's claim to be healed by Jesus may appear to some to be a paradox. Why would Rose, an Orthodox Jew, embrace Jesus, the God of her oppressor, Adolf Hitler? It is indeed an enigma to some that Rose after suffering in five concentration camps as a child, losing her entire family except for her sister and aunt to Adolf's death camps, and knowing of the genocide of six million Jews and some historians quote five million non-Jews would embrace and believe in Jesus, the same God of her oppressor.

Furthermore, how do you come to grips and make sense of a government ruled by an autocrat that enacted laws that were designed to destroy and wipe you off the face of the Earth in the name of ethnic cleansing? This is the question that Rose, her family, fellow Jews, and non-Jews, including Romanis, Christian Poles, communists, homosexuals, Soviet POWs, and the mentally and physically disabled had to faced and answer.

Ironic as it appears, Rose became a Messianic Jew. I reached out to Ms. Price via U.S. Mail to get an update on her claim and to ask some in-depth questions on why she became a "Jew for Jesus." According to Messianic Jews, Jesus (or *Yeshua* in Aramaic), was the Messiah, and he died on behalf of the world's sins. They also believe that the Jews are the chosen people, and that the explicit laws of the Torah, such as observing Shabbat, holidays, and circumcision must be obeyed today.

I did not receive a return response. Sadly, I found out that that she passed away on May 16, 2015 prior to the publication of this book. *Rose Price's Holocaust Journey* is stated below verbatim directly from her website as follows:

> I am a survivor of Hitler's Holocaust. My family lived in a little city in Poland. My upbringing was very Orthodox. My mother instilled in me that Judaism was life. Mealtime was family time. Father would come home from synagogue and recite the Kaddish, the blessing over the wine and the challah, and then he would bless the children. Saturday morning we would go to synagogue, and pick up our afternoon meal of cholent from the bakery, and go enjoy a Sabbath meal around Grandmother's table.
>
> When Hitler took power, change came quickly. We were told, 'Don't come back to the school anymore, because you are Jews.' I was just ten and a half. The Germans threw us out of our homes and put us into a ghetto. Our whole town of Jews was put on one street.

At first I would still pray. When my prayers were not answered, I concluded there was no God. I was transferred from one concentration camp to another until I was sent to Bergen-Belsen and then Dachau. We were tortured. We were put in a field and forced to dig beets out of the almost frozen ground with our bare hands. Our hands bled terribly. All we used to receive was a very thin piece of bread, mostly of sawdust, and a cup of coffee. That was our food for a 24-hour period. I decided I was going to steal a beet and eat it.

When the guard caught me, I got such a bad beating, that even today when I talk about it, I can still feel the cat o' nine tails on my back and face.

The cold weather alone killed many of us. We would have to stand for hours in the snow, half naked and without shoes. One time while we were lined up, we were completely undressed for an experiment to see how long it would take for our blood to freeze. The only reason I survived the experiment was because several people fell on top of me and their bodies kept me warm.

But there were days when I thought I wasn't going to make it. Death looked better than life. I did not know the Lord at that time. I thought I was suffering because He put me in there.

When we were finally liberated in May 1945, I

was full of unforgiveness for what I had been through. The unforgiveness literally poisoned my body, causing me to need 27 operations.

I came to America, married and had children. Although I hated God, I became active in the synagogue. But I was dead inside. I did not believe in God, but I believed in maintaining my Jewish identity and tradition.

One day my teenage daughter came to me and said the worst thing I could imagine. She said, 'I believe in Jesus Christ and He is the Jewish Messiah.' I nearly had a heart attack. I told her what Jesus Christ did to her family. The Nazi guards told me over and over that because I killed Jesus Christ, He hated me and put me into the camps to kill me. When I was seven, I was hit in the head with a crucifix by a priest in Poland for the 'crime' of walking on the sidewalk in front of his church.

My husband became a Believer, too. My younger daughter was still going to a private Hebrew school, but somehow I knew that she had secretly become a Messianic Believer. I was ready to leave my family, but I couldn't. I had already lost my first family under Hitler… all because of this Jesus.

I ran to the rabbi. At the urging of my family, I asked the rabbi about Isaiah 53. He said, 'No Jew reads that.' I asked him about Psalm 22. There are 328 prophecies about the suffering servant Messiah. I asked him about almost all of them.

Finally, the rabbi told me not to come to the synagogue anymore.

So I started sneaking down to the basement and reading the New Testament in a locked room. I read Matthew and it showed me Jesus was a gentle man. He wasn't a killer of my people.

I went to another rabbi, who was also unable to help me. Shortly after that I went to a man's home who was a wealthy Christian businessman who would open his home as an outreach to Jewish people. He asked me if I minded if he prayed for me. 'It's your house, I don't care if you stand on your head,' I told him.

He started to pray, and all of a sudden I closed my eyes and said a very simple prayer: 'God of Abraham, Isaac and Jacob, if it's true, if He is Your Son, as they are saying, and He really is the Messiah, okay. But, Father, if He isn't, forget that I talked to you.' That was the first prayer I had prayed since 1942. I felt the biggest stone rolling off my back. For the first time since the war, I cried and I felt so clean. I knew He was real and I made Him my Messiah.

When Holocaust survivors get angry with me because I am a Messianic Jew, I just show love to them because I know how they feel. I've been there. (99)

Rose's story is indeed remarkable. Many would say it is unbelievable how the power of an unseen force could transform the darkened, desolate, and bruised heart of an individual whose entire family except for her sister and aunt never came out of the death camps. Why did Rose change her theology which for her was also her way of life? How does the psyche make sense of unconscionable and God-forsaken acts that her relatives, fellow Jews, and non-Jews suffered? Approximately eleven million innocent individuals were killed! Why for the first time since 1942 did she feel the biggest stone roll off her back? Why for the first time since the war (and Dachau), was she able to cry and feel clean? On the subject of forgiveness Rose stated the following on her website:

> Forgiveness? I believe in miracles. I believe the Lord performed one of these miracles when He sent me back to Germany as a speaker for 'Berlin for Jesus '81.' I spoke to over 37,000 German people about forgiveness.
>
> Why is this such a miracle? Let me give you an idea of what it was like for me. When I was first asked to speak, my reaction was one of horror. For anyone to ask me to set foot on the land where my family was extinguished was more than I could bear. I was torn between obeying the Lord and holding on to my bitterness and hate; the Lord finally won. The miracle was that God spoke through me in Germany about Romans 8:1 and Matthew 6:12-15, scriptures speaking of forgiveness.
>
> But even more importantly, He healed my hurting heart and ministered to many others. After I spoke, six ex-Nazi soldiers came up to me and asked me to forgive them; one even

> told me he was a guard in the camp where I was. If God saw fit to forgive them, who was I not to forgive. God is, indeed, a miracle working God! (99)

It is truly amazing how the power of Jesus Christ through the Word of God and fellow believers ministered to Rose. According to Rose, gone are the need for her to endure continuous operations and to daily experience anger, hatred, and self-loathing. Rose, while alive (like Saul who initially persecuted Christians and then took up the banner of Christianity), dedicated her life to letting Jews and Gentiles know that Jesus is alive, real, and he is the Messiah Yeshua (Jesus), the savior of the world; to the Jew first, and also to the Gentile.

During her life Rose spoke often to groups about her Holocaust experiences and her faith in Jesus. Her website is still active at RosePriceMinistries.org (99). She is also the author of the DVD, *Rose Price: Holocaust, Journey to Forgiveness*, which is available online. Her story is also available on YouTube (100).

Up until her death, Rose, hurt by oppressive, inhumane German fathers, leaders, and authorities, declared boldly that she had been healed by God. While alive, she proclaimed the good news of Jesus and spoke at churches, synagogues, and both public and private schools in the United States. She was a featured speaker at "Berlin for Jesus" and in Nuremberg at the Anniversary of Hitler's proclamation. She was also an honored guest in Canada, Poland, Jamaica, Honduras, Costa Rica, Guatemala and Puerto Rico.

Chapter 8

Albert, "Ashamed of Who I Am"

Healed from American Genocide

Manifest Destiny (99) is a term for the attitude prevalent during the 19th century period of American expansion that the United States not only could, but was destined to, even divinely ordained to stretch from coast to coast. This attitude helped expand western settlement, Native American removal and sparked the war with Mexico. Manifest Destiny imposed on Native Americans resulted in the genocide of approximately 99 percent of their population according to a YouTube documentary entitled, *The Wellbriety Journey to Forgiveness* (100). Although there was a very small minority of dissenters to this belief in Manifest Destiny, there were far too many individuals who believed that this was the right course of action for the United States.

After independence had been won in the Revolutionary War and reaffirmed in the War of 1812, the spirit of nationalism that swept the nation in the next two decades demanded more territory. This was fueled by President Andrew Jackson's, "every man is equal" mentality. Now, with territory up to the Mississippi River claimed and settled and the Louisiana Purchase explored, Americans headed west in droves. The term, "Manifest Destiny" was coined in 1845 by newspaper editor John O'Sullivan to describe the essence of this mindset (99).

One of the central messages of Manifest Destiny was that darkness and ignorance would be replaced with civilization. This sentiment was propelled as well by the religious fervor of the Second Great Awakening (99). This evangelical move was a shift to an emphasis on the ordinary person's ability to change their situation for the better. It emphasized that individuals could exercise free will in choosing to be saved and suggested that salvation was open to all human beings including women and blacks. This more optimistic view of the human condition opened the door for greater public roles for white women and much higher African-American participation in Christianity than ever before.

Many settlers believed that God himself had blessed the growth of the American nation. At that time, the Native Americans as well as African Americans were considered heathens. By Christianizing the tribes, American missionaries believed they could save souls and they became among the first to cross the Mississippi River.

Paintings like *American Progress*, (circa 1872 by John Gast) were used to symbolize the modernization of the new west by leading American settlers westward. In the painting, *Columbia*, a personification of the United States, appears as a female angel and is shown stringing telegraph wire with her left hand as she sweeps west. In her right hand she holds a school book symbolizing enlightenment to the heathens and uneducated.

Lyrics in the song, *America the Beautiful*, by Katharine Lee Bates— "God shedding His grace…from sea to shining sea; pilgrim feet… across the wilderness; and May God thy gold refine Till all success be nobleness, And every gain divine"— pronounced the virtue, rewards, and fruits of Manifest Destiny. The words from this poem were later turned into an American patriotic song which approved and sanctioned the westward expansion. The repetition of *America, America* in each stanza further implored God to continue to bless America and her patriots.

At the heart of Manifest Destiny was the pervasive belief in the cultural and racial superiority of Caucasian Americans. Native Americans had long been perceived as inferior, and efforts to civilize them had been widespread since the days of John Smith and Miles Standish. The Hispanics who ruled Texas and the lucrative ports of California were also seen as backward.

Today, many Native Americans have banded together and formed *The Wellbriety Journey to Forgiveness* documentary project to tell the story of the effects of Manifest Destiny and to bring healing to the descendants of the remaining 1 percent (99 percent were victims of genocide) of Native Americans. In this video documentary by Don Coy their story is told of genocide, abuse, sterilization, forced separations and boarding schools, beatings, rape, dehumanization, which have led to the current situation of self-hatred, alcoholism, poverty, intergenerational trauma, and cultural eradication among Native Americans.

History books record it as assimilation, an attempt to save the remaining 1 percent of the Native American population, but the descendants, those that survive this period, tell a different story in this documentary. They purport that at the heart of the issue was the forced separation and placement of Native American children in 500 boarding schools across the country in an attempt to annihilate the remaining 1 percent of the population by cultural assimilation.

Albert White Hat, a Lakota Native American is one of the featured individuals who shares his story in the documentary. Albert and his fellow Native Americans' accounts of this gut-wrenching attempt to dehumanize and obliterate them from the planet are painful to hear and watch. The generational abuse they experienced is contrasted by the fragility of their spirit to persevere against all odds and assert their humanity is spite of being repeatedly victimized by their oppressors.

Albert White Hat as an adult vividly recalled the anger and fury he experienced when he came to grips with the realty of the effects of Manifest Destiny and Indian boarding schools. Native Americans now refer to this aftermath as "intergenerational trauma" inflicted upon them by U.S. laws, policies, and churches as children. In the video, Albert recalls how his healing was brought about by a reliving of and a cathartic release from the past abuses towards him and Native Americans.

In the late '60s, Albert returned to his native land, let his hair grow out, and began to retreat to the hills for solace. Alone, one night during a fast at midnight after praying, he had flashbacks about the atrocities, policies, and laws committed by the U.S. Government and churches against him and the Lakotas. As he replayed each event in his mind, he became consumed with anger that exploded over into hatred to the point that he wanted to do a mass killing of white Americans.

Looking at the whole picture, he felt that if he did this, his grandfathers would honor him.

As he got up and faced the magnificent eastern skyline, the beautiful stars, the rolling hills, the outline of the moon and the morning star, he changed his mind and made a decision to live. In the midst of such peace and beauty, he reasoned that *if he did not forgive, he would end up dead*, either from alcoholism or putting a gun to his head. He instead exploded in tears and chose to forgive in order to be happy and live. Albert explains in the video that he now has to pray every day for strength to forgive his oppressors. He further explains that this dilemma is something that will be with the Lakotas for the next 100-200 years and each one of them will have to make a decision to forgive and live, or face self destruction.

Dr. Raymond Reyes, also featured in the documentary, has studied Native American children caught up in the foster care system and has seen the vestiges of more than five generations of intergenerational trauma. He believes that this inability to properly parent originated from broken homes as a result of children being institutionalized in boarding schools. Dr. Reyes makes a comparison of this trauma to the Jewish Holocaust, but he laments that after more than five generations of this treatment, Native Americans do not have an Anne Frank or Schindler's List to tell their story. The agony for the Lakotas he states is that there are not any history books or anecdotal accounts to share the truth with the world so that healing and reconciliation can take place.

Today, Albert White Hat is on the path to wholeness. He has been hurt by American founding fathers, and is finding healing now in God. Albert admits that for him his healing is progressing and the effort of forgiveness must be practiced daily for him to be free from past hurts and abuses. He has channeled his hurt and pain into *The Wellbriety Journey to Forgiveness* project.

The mission of this project is to tell the story that the history books don't tell about the genocidal effects of Manifest Destiny and the resultant intergenerational trauma. Their goal is to bring about healing by using forgiveness, spirituality, and Indian culture to establish restoration and reconciliation. Across the United States they are now implementing plans to have Grief Recovery Coaches in all communities in order to help those suffering from the effects of American genocidal policies and intergenerational trauma. Complimentary DVD copies of the video can be obtained from www.whitebison.org. Their email address is: info@whitebison.org.

Chapter 9

Yours Truly Joyce, "Nobody Loves Me"

Healed from Domestic Violence

When my father and my mother forsake me, then the Lord will take me up. Psalm 27:10

I feel transparency is an important part of the healing process in the lives of individuals. I was advised by an attorney not to show my flaws and to tell of my wounds. Needless to say, I choose to take my advice from the master counselor himself, Jesus, the Great Physician- the one who knows all, sees all, is the creator of the universe, and has the power of life and death in his hands. These are the same hands that doubting Thomas wanted to see and place his own hands, that is, in Jesus' nail holes and in his pierced side.

The act of Jesus granting Thomas' request caused him to believe. Likewise, I feel it is necessary to be transparent and show my wounds in the hope that individuals will hear my story and be set free. Regardless of the embarrassment or pain it may personally cause me, I feel it is expedient that I do so in order that the bruised and broken-hearted know that they too can be healed.

Reflecting back on my years with my father I can say I loved him without a doubt in spite of his many imperfections. Although I tried to be the apple of his eye, thinking I could change him, it was useless. I felt I had no choice but to tolerate and hate some of his abusive ways while he was alive. Like Pastor Donnie (Chapter Six), I grew up continuously trying to arbitrate and break up my parents' fights.

As I grew older, I would hold my breath hoping that I wouldn't come home and encounter my parents in the middle of an argument. The possible embarrassment of hearing my mom called abusive names or seeing vivid red, black, and blue bruises on her light skin was not a pretty sight. Stamped in my memory which I have never forgotten, is the sight of my dad pulling my mom down the project stairs. I hated to see the pain in my mom's eyes and her sense of helplessness. I loved both my parents dearly and even though my dad should not have physically or verbally abused mom, I didn't think it was right for her to retaliate by spitting in his food or drink and then serving it to him.

Scenes like this were extremely difficult for me as a child to witness especially between the two parents that I loved. The act of seeing them inflict abuse on each other was very painful to watch, recall, and to now write about it. Somehow I had to come to grips with circumstances that I had no control over. It was extremely frustrating and though it happened right before my eyes, I wanted to deny with all my might that it was occurring. The best way I can describe it is to say that the sense of loss of control made me feel as if my life was ending. It left me as a child feeling hopeless, depressed, and fearful.

I feared that one or both of my parents would get seriously hurt, or possibly die. I also feared that my mom might instead of putting saliva in my dad's food, might put something more deadly in it. My dad definitely had an anger management problem, but he also had a gun that he kept in the house. As a former expert rifleman in the military, I knew he definitely knew how to shoot to kill. This dysfunctional behavior and lifestyle stopped me from bringing friends over, particularly on the weekends. I knew it would be all hell if my dad lost money at the race-tracks, was angry about something that didn't go his way, or had too much to drink.

One manifestation of my dad's vitriolic anger has never left me. I can vividly recall my oldest brother, Del, getting beaten with dad's leather razor belt because he lost my dad's barber tools. Frantically, I banged on Del's bedroom door and pleaded for my dad to stop beating him, but to no avail. However, I never accepted that it was okay for my dad to inflict such pain. The punishment never fit the crime in my mind. I feared that belt and to this day, I still get a visceral response when I see a belt in someone's hand. It conjures up memories of Del calling out for mercy and past fears that are difficult to put into words.

Although, at that time many parents beat their children with belts, ironing cords, and switches, I never truly accepted that it was okay. For the most part I always empathized with the abused individual and felt that the punishment was unmerited and too severe.

Parenthetically, it was not uncommon for my friends and class-mates to come to school with multiple severe bruises and whelps on their bodies. Some parents would actually come to school and beat their children in the students' closet over an infraction.

Around the age of thirteen, which is when I gave my life to Christ, I can recall babysitting for the neighbor's children. The parents gave me a belt and instructed me to beat their kids with it if they misbehaved. Honestly, I tried using the belt lightly a few times, but decided I would not use this type of discipline. I chose instead to verbally speak to the children in order to correct any misbehavior.

At that time there were not many laws, if any to protect kids. Corporeal punishment was inflicted by not only parents, but others in authority, like teachers. The consensus at that time seemed to be that if you got severely beat, you were bad and deserved it. Not only did kids experience corporeal punishment at school, but when they got home they would get beat again.

Nowadays, I hear many comedians joke and laugh as they recall these experiences, but they never talk about the damaged emotional psyches or the physical scars that remained. Unfortunately, many children were beat at school and at home for having learning disabilities and special needs which impeded their ability to learn. Some were even made to sit in a corner or wear a dunce hat because they were deemed stupid and uneducable by their teachers.

Returning to my experiences with my dad, as I grew older I came to accept his abusive nature. I had no choice but to. However, I do recall one time as a child devising a plan to run away from home because I felt that no one loved me. Looking back I don't know whether it was sibling rivalry over the birth of my brother who is five years my junior, frustration with my sister because she had a severe case of eczema and had to be constantly placated and favored, or frustration with living in a hostile, depressing environment.

Whatever the reason, when I cried out my dad told me he loved me and I decided against running away because I didn't want to live in the streets. At that time we lived in the projects and I was well aware of classmates who begged me at lunch for my Spam sandwiches that I couldn't stomach. I chose to stay, but I was cognizant of how other families functioned and I was always drawn towards friends who had more sane familial relationships. One family in particular, was Audrey Compton's who like Laurie's special family (Chapter Three), offered me a respite from the dysfunction I experienced in my own home. During high school, Audrey's family always had an open door for me and allowed me to stay overnight on the weekends.

Two other major transformative events that positively impacted me and later my family was my receipt of a scholarship to Palfrey Street School, a private high school and a six year scholarship to Simmons College in Boston, Massachusetts. Upon graduation from Simmons, I was awarded a master's degree in psychiatric social work. Once I entered college, I was basically home-free because Simmons provided free tuition, room and board, and a stipend.

Interestingly enough, it was my dad who encouraged me to take the four year scholarship to Palfrey. I was reluctant to go because it meant I had to travel an hour by bus, two trains, and a trolley each way to get back and forth to school. He told me it was "a golden opportunity" so I took a chance which later forever changed my life and that of my family's. Although these external promotions were life changing, the internal damage my dad did to my siblings' and my psyche are difficult to enumerate and elaborate on in writing.

But I will share a few to let the reader know that his abuse was not specific to any child. He constantly told my oldest brother, Del, that he wouldn't amount to anything even though Del had a college degree. After Del attempted suicide following his divorce in his late twenties, my dad allowed him to return home, but didn't want him to take medication for his depression. My dad fed into Del's paranoia by telling him that you could not trust psychiatrists, especially if they were white.

My brother, Joe, who also has mental problems, was told by my paternal uncle, dad's only brother, that he and Del were wasted seeds. This same uncle told my dad I must have moved to Atlanta because I was gay and didn't want anyone in the family to know it.

My dad constantly blamed my mother for my sister's eczema and said that when my mother carried my sister in utero my mother's diet caused it, even though he himself had dry scaly skin and my mom had soft, creamy skin. My youngest brother, Rob, the baby was spared some of the abuse from my dad because Rob was born when dad was in his forties. But he too can recall episodes of coming home and encountering our parents in spirited and physically abusive arguments.

Once when my dad visited me in Atlanta he bought me a bed and later told me I should have relations with someone. At the time, I was in my mid-thirties and he told me that it would be terrible if I became an old maid and didn't have any children. I would not call my dad a misogynist, but he did have some extreme biased views on the roles of women and men and how they should interact with each other. For example, after my sister had a hysterectomy, he told her that no man would want her.

Even though I moved to Atlanta in my late twenties, I would continuously awaken in the middle of the night. I knew instinctively to pray a prayer of protection over my mom that no harm or danger would come to her. Before moving some of my siblings and I tried to do an intervention with both parents, but it was useless. My dad, a former World War II army sergeant was all powerful. His voice was stronger, forceful, and more powerful than ours. We were in Garnett B. Farrar's house that he had worked for and paid for with a third grade education. Although all five siblings had attended or finished college, it didn't matter- it was his house and we were his kids. As far as he was concerned we may have had book knowledge, but we didn't know anything about life or relationships.

When Rob confronted him once on his behavior, my dad told him that Rob came from "his nuts," which translated meant dad, the progenitor would always be right. My dad was not changing and he had my mom so threatened and afraid, she would not dare leave him.

My dad was diagnosed with terminal prostate cancer in 2001 and was given about six months to live. For the most part I was left to care for my parents' needs. I was exhausted and had little help from my siblings. One morning, I got up early and brought breakfast to my parents. My husband told me I was neglecting our family and my siblings should help out. Against my husband's wishes and risking damage to our marriage, I went. My dad's appetite was declining and he ate very little of the meal that I brought for him and mom. He also complained that I had brought it to them late and told me to put it to the dresser drawer. I questioned why the dresser drawer instead of the refrigerator, and he told me so that Del wouldn't eat it. My dad then instructed me in a gruff manner to get him some milk to drink.

At this point I was exhausted, depressed, and felt unappreciated even by my own husband. As I poured the milk, I heard God say to me in a still small voice, "As often as you do this, do this in remembrance of me." I broke into tears. I had always heard and understood this verse in relation to taking communion and remembering Christ's sacrifice on the cross for us. I now understood that God was telling me that someone has to love the unlovables, to turn the other cheek, and offer compassion even to someone I might perceive as being undeserving. I understood that he was revealing to me that he loved me and saw the sacrifices I was making for family members in spite of their mistreatment of me.

In retrospect, although I was trained as a psychotherapist and received individual counseling from a private therapist, I attribute my healing to the redemptive saving power of Christ in my life. Therapy definitely helped me to sort through some emotional issues of self-esteem, self-worth, my identity as an African American female, and career goals. However, for the deep levels of abuse, hatred, unforgiveness, and self-worth, the healing balm for me came from the word of God. By submitting my life to Christ I experienced a personal revelation of God; a forgiveness of my sins. I learned the merits of and the meaning of the scripture that tells us to pray for and forgive our enemies.

By doing so, I experienced a sense of wholeness. Against all odds- even my therapist doubted that I could make it in Atlanta on my own, without any family, and only having one classmate from undergraduate school as a friend— I was able to stand, survive, and thrive. Like Joseph, I eventually became the conduit for all my family members to move to Atlanta, even my elderly and stricken parents. As Joseph provided for his family members, I have been able to care for my two disabled brothers on an ongoing basis. I was also able to care for my mom in the advanced stages of Alzheimer's disease and my dad during the final stages of terminal prostate cancer.

I no longer see myself as a victim, but a victor in Christ. I know that I am fearfully and wonderfully made up of an estimated 37.2 trillion cells by God. I believe his Word that says that I am the head and not the tail! I am no longer concerned about hatred, jealousy, sexism, racism, sickness, or poverty. God has been a present help and a provider in my life. He has answered my prayers and opened doors that others said would be barred to me. God has given me the desires of my heart and blessed me with a wonderful loving husband and provider, Tillmon H. Rosemon Jr. Although we have had some heated disagreements, we have never had any domestic violence in our marriage of more than 23 years.

At the age of 42, following the stillbirth of our daughter, Tiffany, and two miscarriages, God blessed us with our beloved son, David. He is now a junior in college, has studied abroad, and is a member of The National Society of Collegiate Scholars. Prior to his birth, I was told I was too old to have a child, but I heard God's confirmation in my spirit as follows: *Is there anything too hard for God? Look at my daughter Sarah. If I blessed her and she was much older than you, shall I not do the same? My promise to you is to give you the desires of your heart. When your mother and father forsake you, then will I take you up. Ask and it shall be given, seek and you will find, knock and the door shall be open. I am the great I am! I open doors that no man can shut, and what I shut no one can open.*

Another miracle happened in my life approximately two or three weeks prior to my dad's death. On that day, he called me into his room and asked that I forgive him. It was so sudden and it had occurred after being at my dad's beck and call with little or no signs of appreciation. Of course I agreed to, but I don't think he knew that I had already forgiven him a long time ago. It would have been to my detriment if I had not. I would have continued to be the victim; carrying pain, anger, and depression that would have kept me in bondage. If I had held on to unforgiveness, I would probably not have experienced the gains I have made in my life.

If I had not forgiven him a long time ago, the hatred for my dad probably would have been transferred onto men and produced some negative and dysfunctional relationships. Forgiving my dad and God's healing me through his word gave me strength to love, persevere, and take risks; believing that God was my vindicator and redeemer. He fulfilled his promise to open doors for me, show me favor, make me the head and not the tail, and give me the desires of my heart. As I delighted in him and obeyed his word, he was faithful to it and granted me the desires of my heart.

In summary, in my heart or maybe it was from watching too many *Father Knows Best* or *Hazel* episodes, I have always been drawn as a young child to help hurting people. I have always had what they call a tender heart and a spirit of reconciliation. I could cry on a dime, almost for no reason at all. Looking back, I'm sure that is why I pursued psychiatric social work in college, currently run empowerment groups for hurting people, and why I have become an author of several self-help books.

I now understand that the pain, dysfunction and the abuses I suffered were for a purpose which I now use through the power of God's word to redeem others who are in bondage to abuse, molestation, generational and societal curses, and misguided parenting. Through my suffering I have learned that my mission is to fulfill the tenets found in Hebrews 12:12-13, "Therefore, strengthen your feeble arms and weak knees. Make level paths for your feet, *so that the lame may not be disabled, but rather healed.*" My goal, like the other respondents in this anthology, is to help those who were lame at birth, *hurt by their fathers*, or through generational curses, misguided parenting, or societal abuses become *healed* through the power of God's word.

EPILOGUE

"Where Do We Go From Here?"

Thou art the helper of the fatherless. Psalm 10:14

Manifest Destiny, Survival of the Fittest; - are these justifications for not being our brother's keeper? We have examined the lives of nine individuals including myself who have suffered abuse, violence, and aggression at the hands of parents, authority figures, governments, or institutional systems that have practiced racism, sexism, genocide, greed, and hatred. Oftentimes these heinous deeds were even done in the name of God to justify their hideous and unspeakable actions.

These hurt and abused individuals all chose not to follow in the footsteps of their oppressors. Like lambs going to the slaughter, they did not go. They believed in their hearts the words of the past theologian Theodore Parker, paraphrased by Dr. Martin Luther King that, "The arc of the moral universe is long, but it bends toward justice." In Dr. King's August 16, 1967 speech entitled, "*Where Do We Go From Here?*", faced with a patriarchal society that practiced aggression in the form of institutional racism, sexism, genocide, and fratricide at home and abroad, Dr. King offered love as a solution to his listeners. In a sermon he wrote while in jail for committing nonviolent civil disobedience during the Montgomery bus boycott, he also offered forgiveness as a solution and explained its connectivity to love in the face of oppression by answering a rhetorical question as follows: "How do we love our enemies? First, we must develop and maintain the capacity to forgive. He who is devoid of the power to forgive is devoid of the power to love" (100).

Almost five decades later Professor Stephen Hawking, Ph.D. addressed this same issue of aggression during a personal guided tour of London's Science Museum. In response to a question asked him about what human shortcomings he would most like to alter, Dr. Hawking, regarded as one of the most brilliant theoretical physicists in history, gave the following response: "The human failing I would most like to correct is aggression. It may have had survival advantage in caveman days, to get more food, territory, or partner with whom to reproduce, but now it threatens to destroy us all. A major nuclear war would be the end of civilization, and may be the end of the human race. The quality I would most like to magnify is empathy. It brings us together in a peaceful, loving state."

Dr. Hawking offered empathy, which the dictionary defines as, "the psychological identification with or vicarious experiencing of the feelings, thoughts, or attitudes of another" as the solution to mankind's aggressive and abusive nature. The hope is that if we see our brother or sister as ourselves, then we won't destroy them or turn in on ourselves and self-destruct. If we see them as ourselves in other words, we will offer healing by forgiving and restoring them back to wholeness.

Almost 50 years later, I now reiterate Dr. King's poignant question— "Where do we go from here?" I would trump this question by adding two more, which are just as pressing, if not more, which are: What should be the role of a father and authority figures in our world? And secondly, how do we handle the aggression that Dr. Hawking mentioned which now threatens to cause the demise of mankind and the world?

The dictionary has various definitions of the word father and the roles that they play in society. Webster defines father as follows: "a male parent, a father-in-law, stepfather, or adoptive father, any male ancestor, especially the founder of a family or line; a man who exercises paternal care over other persons; a father to the poor, to assume as one's own; to perform the tasks or duties of a male parent."

These definitions by and large have a positive, life affirming connotation attached to them. They dictate that fathers should be the creators of actions that promote and protect life. It speaks of action taken by men that are noteworthy and of good repute. In contrast, how do we handle this aggression that threatens to destroy mankind and at the same time protect the next generation by providing children with fathers and authority figures that affirm and watch over them?

A quick glance at crime statistics seem to tell a dismal story- Men commit more acts of violence than women. The U.S. Department of Justice sponsored a National Crime Victimization Study in 2007. This evaluation found that 75.6 percent of all offenders were male and only 20.1 percent were female (99). These statistics are noteworthy because for every male that is incarcerated, the potential number of absentee or fatherless homes rises.

According to the 2011 U.S. Census Bureau data, over 24 million, that is one out of every three (33 percent) children in America and nearly two in three (63 percent) African American children live in homes without the presence of a father (99).

David Popenoe, a professor of sociology at Rutgers University, states that:

> The decline of fatherhood is a major force behind many of the most disturbing problems that plague American society: crime and delinquency; teenage pregnancy; deteriorating educational achievement; depression, substance abuse, and alienation among adolescents; and the growing number of women and children living in poverty. The current generation of children may be the first in our nation's history to be less well off—psychologically, socially, economically, and morally—than their parents were at the same age (99).

Popenoe goes on to say that if present trends continue "nearly 50 percent of American children may be going to sleep each evening without being able to say good night to their dads" (99). Consequently, for every absent father, a child by definition is potentially left without a male parent to watch over and protect the next generation from abuse, delinquency, drug use, teenage pregnancy, dropping out of high school, and other social ills. All of the individuals in this anthology by definition fell into this category of having an absentee father, physically and/or emotionally. As a result, they were not adequately affirmed, valued, or protected and were left prey to the negative elements of society mentioned above.

They say there is nothing new under the sun. If we search the Bible we can also find examples of the effects of fatherlessness on children and their mothers. One of the earliest occurrences was between Abraham and his concubine, Hagar, the mother of their son Ishmael. Hagar was so distressed that she wanted to end her life and that of her son because Abraham abandoned them and told her to leave his household.

But God intervened in the form of an angel as he did for the individuals in this book, and prophesized to Hagar that although Ishmael would become a wild seed, meaning he wouldn't amount to anything without a father in the home to protect him, God had commanded a blessing over his life. Hagar was instructed to return to her mistress (the oppressive situation) and he would watch over and protect her by making Ishmael's descendants too numerous to count. She was also instructed to name him Ishmael, which means, the "Lord has heard of your misery."

I believe that we can, must, and should intervene and put an end to this epidemic of abuse and suffering that has been fostered by fathers, authority figures, and institutions not being on their post. I believe that God wants us to be Good Samaritans and use our ears, hearts, and hands to provide the love, guidance, and protection for fatherless children in oppressive situations. The *Wellbriety Movement: Journey to Forgiveness* mentioned in Chapter Eight is an excellent start on a grass roots level. This project can also be duplicated and customized for non-Native American communities.

Secular and religious institutions can also develop new and enhance their current programs that address the needs of those who have been abused and left without the protection of a father. There is no excuse for not being our brother's keeper. If social, governmental programs are not working, fix them and make them cost effective. Put in checks and balances to make sure they are properly utilized to exclude waste, abuse, fraud, and mishandling of public and private funds.

We as human beings can learn from the past, exercise empathy that Dr. Hawking mentions and declare a cost efficient *war on fatherlessness and aggression.* These are two social ills that threaten to end mankind and the world as we now know it. If we don't address this crisis, then we curse ourselves and the next generation. As with Hagar, so with Abel, as with those who have been abused— their pain, their blood cries out to God and he hears our pain (Genesis 4:10-12). Manifest Destiny, Survival of the Fittest— these can never be justifications for not being our brother's keeper.

It has often been stated that, "The only thing necessary for the triumph of evil is for good men to do nothing." We are commanded in the very first chapter of the Bible to be fruitful, multiply, and replenish the earth and have authority over every living thing. We are also instructed in Isaiah 32 that if we want peace in our cities, joy in our homes and the end of destruction within our families, we must pursue justice and righteousness. In other words, in order to bless future generations, fathers and authority figures must step up and fulfill their role as benevolent progenitors in our society for lasting peace to take place in our world for generations to come.

In summary, for those who have been hurt by their fathers and/or authority figures, the good news is that your healing awaits you! God hears and knows of your suffering as he did with Hagar's. As he healed her and the individuals in this anthology, (including myself) God stands with open arms waiting to heal you. The individuals featured in this book received their healing through the grace of God by practicing forgiveness, love, and following the word of God. Like Hagar they endured their oppressive situations and God delivered them in spite of fathers and authority figures not being on their post.

Finally, although God is a healer, this does not let society off the hook however and serve as an excuse for not being our brother's keeper. In this modern age, unchecked aggression and the *survival of the fittest* mentality cannot coexist with man being an intelligent being. It is an outdated oxymoron that will lead to our demise by being wise fools in our own eyes. Much of the human suffering in the world today can be eliminated by fathers and authority figures being on their post, Good Samaritans that act as brother's keepers, and short-term, cost effective secular and religious programs and institutions that combat the causes of aggression and fatherlessness.

APPENDIX

(Note to the reader: Detailed on the following pages are national resources for individuals trying to overcome loneliness, depression, discrimination, barrenness, abuse, and other self-destructive behaviors. This list is by no means exhaustive, but it is an attempt to identify resources found in most major cities across the United States. The author is not affiliated with and does not personally endorse any of these organizations, and is not responsible or liable for any of its services or products.)

RESOURCES

RESOURCES AND HELP FOR INDIVIDUALS DEALING WITH LONELINESS, DEPRESSION, RUNAWAYS & MISSING PERSONS	
Counseling Center	www.couns.uiuc.edu/brochures/lone ine.htm
Walking-Wounded.Net (Christian based)	www.walking-wounded.net
Self-Help Support Groups for Older Women by Lenard W. Kaye	http://books.google.com/books
Crisis Helpline (for any kind of crisis)	(800) 233-4357
Youth Crisis Hotline	(866) 4-U-TREVOR
Common Ground Sanctuary	(800) 231-1127
Crisis Line for the Handicapped	(888) 711-TEEN
National Child – At Risk Hotline	(800) FOR A CHILD
National Runaway Switchboard	(800) 621-4000
National Youth Crisis Hotline (Christian Based)	(800) 448-4663
Depression/Alcohol and Drug Addiction Hotline	(800) 861-1768
National Hopeline Network (Suicide Prevention)	(800) 784-2433
National Runaway Switchboard	(800) RUNAWAY
Covenant House "Nineline"	(800) 999-9999
National Center for Missing & Exploited Children	(800) 843-5678
National Runaway for the Hearing Impaired	(800) 621-0394 (TDD)
Child Find of America	(800) 426-5678

RESOURCES AND HELP FOR INDIVIDUALS DEALING WITH SEXUAL, DOMESTIC, DRUG, CHEMICAL ABUSE, & OTHER DISORDERS	
National Domestic Violence Hotline	(800) 799-7233
National Child Abuse Hotline	(800) FOR A CHILD
Divorce Care	(800) 268-1343
National Counsel on Child Abuse & Family Violence	(800) 222-2000
National Herpes Hotline	(800) 232-4636
Rape & Abuse & Incest National Network	(800) 656-HOPE
National Domestic Violence Hotline	(800) 799-7233
Psychiatric and Substance Abuse Hotline	(800) 331-2900
Al-Anon for Families of Alcoholics	(800) 344-2666
Alcohol and Drug Helpline	(800) 821-4357
Families Anonymous	(800) 736-9805
National Council on Alcoholism and Drug Dependence	(800) 622-2255
Be Sober Hotline	(800) 237-6237
1 800 Alcohol Recovery Center	(800) 2117-6465
Alcohol & Drug Abuse National Clearing House	(800) 729-6686
The American Anorexia/Bulimia Association	(800) 1172-2230
Victim of Crime Help Line	(800) 394-2255
National Center on Elder Abuse Hotline	(800) 677-1116
National Capital Poison Control Center	(800) 222-1222

RESOURCES AND HELP FOR INDIVIDUALS DEALING WITH DISCRIMINATION	
National AIDS Hotline	(800) 342-2437
CDC AIDS Info	(800) 232-4636
The Teen AIDS Hotline	(800) 440-TEEN
National Sexually Transmitted Disease Hotline	(800) 227-8922
AIDS in Prison Project's Hotline	(718) 378-7022
The American with Disabilities Act Information and Assistance	(800) 514-0301
The Gay and Lesbian National Hotline	(888) 843-4564
CDC National Prevention Information Network	(800) 458- 11731
AIDS Info	(800) 448-0440
National Women's Health Resource Center	(877) 986-9472
(NAMI) National Alliance for the Mentally Ill Helpline	(800) 950-6264
Mental Health America	(800) 969-6642
Office for Civil Rights	(800) 368-1019

RESOURCES AND HELP FOR INDIVIDUALS DEALING WITH BARRENNESS, UNDEREMPLOYMENT AND UNEMPLOYMENT	
Planned Parenthood Hotline	(800) 230–71176
The Fertility Institute	(800) 433-9009
American Infertility Association	(888) 917-3777
National Women's Health Information Center	(800) 994-9662
www.literacydirectory.org/	(800) 228-8813
www.careeronestop.org/	(877) 348-0502
www.getthejob.com	Feedback@getthejob.com
www.superpages.com	(800) 376-0136
www.careerbuilder.com	(866) 438-1485
www.employment.com	Info@employment.com
www.snagajob.com	(877) 461-7624
www.jobfox.com	(888) 667-8080

RESOURCES AND HELP FOR INDIVIDUALS DEALING WITH ADDICTIONS AND COMPULSIVE DISORDERS	
Cocaine Anonymous	(800) 347-8998
National Help Line for Substance Abuse	(800) 662-HELP
Drug Abuse Information & Referral Line	(800) 662-4357
AL Anon	(888) 425-2666
Sexual Compulsive Anonymous	(800) 977- HEAL
Sex Addiction Helpline	(866) 464-HEAL
Sexual Addicts Anonymous	(800) 477-8191
Anorexia Nervosa and Associated Disorders	(800) 445-1900
National Eating Disorder Association	(800) 931-2237
Overeater Anonymous	(505) 891-2664
Debtors Anonymous	(781) 453-2743

NOTES

NOTES

BIBLIOGRAPHY

Flemons, Natalie. *From The Chaos To The Call.* Matteson: TLG Printing, Inc. 2009.

Frank, Anne and B.M. Mooyaart. *Anne Frank: The Diary of a Young Girl.* United States: Doubleday & Company, 19117.

Keneally, Thomas. *Schindler's List.* New York: Touchstone, 1993.

McClurkin, Donnie. *Eternal Victim, Eternal Victor.* Lanham: Pneuma Life Publishing, 2001.

Myers, Teresa. *Persecuted Saints Within the Church Wall.* Mustang: Tate Publishing, 2008.

Owens, Leila. *Still Standing.* Columbus: Brentwood Christian Press: 2008.

Plante, Thomas G. Faith and Health: *Psychological Perspectives.* New York: Guilford, 2001.

Smith, Laurie Ann. *A Life of Death: The Redemption.* Alberta: Lulu.com 2011.

WEBSITES

www.bjs.gov/content/pub/pdf/cvus0702.pdf (*Criminal Victimization in the United States, 2007 Statistical Tables National Crime Victimization Survey, Table 38*) Retrieved 9/20/15

www.buzz.eewmagazine.com/eew-magazine-buzz-blog/2012/9/10/donnie-mcclurkin-repairing-broken-relationship-with-12-year.html#ooid=95djl0NToPDnLJBrRCNKNrZSd0Unl6jJ&ootime=19m00s (*Donnie McClurkin Interview*) Retrieved 8/25/15

www.census.gov/prod/2011pubs/p70-126.pdf (*Living Arrangements of Children: 2009*)

Household Economic Studies, (Table 1) Retrieved 9/20/15

www.jewishvoice.org/who-is-yeshua/jews-who-believed/rose-price.html (*Rose Price's Holocaust Journey*) Retrieved 8/22/15

rosepriceministries.org/ (*Forgiveness*) Retrieved 8/22/15

www.blogtalkradio.com/inspirationalvoices (*Inspirational Voices)* Retrieved 7/29/15

www.blogtalkradio.com/laurie-smith (*Laurie Ann Smith BlogTalk Radio*) Retrieved 5/23/15

www.ushistory.org/us/22c.asp (*The Second Great Awakening*) Retrieved 6/15/15

www.ushistory.org/us/29.asp (*Manifest Destiny*) Retrieved 6/15/15

www.utne.com/politics/decline-of-fatherhood-american-nuclear-family.aspx (*The Decline of Fatherhood*: *Disappearing dads are destroying our future*) Retrieved 9/20/15

WEBSITES

www.whitebison.org Retrieved 9/20/15

www.salsa.net/peace/conv/8weekconv4-2.html (*Loving Your Enemies by Martin Luther King, Jr.*) Retrieved 9/20/15

www.youtu.be/hBWH29lJSX0 (*Rose Price Interview*) Retrieved 8/22/15

www.youtu.be/s6zVj3nBmNs (*Where Do We Go From Here - August 16, 1967*) Retrieved 9/20/15

www.youtu.be/vZwF9NnQbWM?t=30s (The *Wellbriety Journey to Forgiveness Documentary*) Retrieved 7/2/15

ABOUT THE AUTHOR

C. Joyce Farrar-Rosemon, BA, MSW, Ed.S. has not only survived, but has thrived after living in a home where domestic violence was rampart. In addition, she has overcome poverty, abuse, loneliness, low self-esteem, depression, job loss, a stillbirth and two miscarriages. In '92 she opened a real estate company with her husband's help in her 7th month of pregnancy with only $10.00 in the operating account that subsequently blossomed into a six figure income. Following the real estate demise in 2007, she went from making six figures- to no figures- and had to survive on various low paying jobs. Finally, after going back to school and filling out over 400 applications she landed a job as a Certified Educator at the age of 57. Joyce speaks frequently to non-profit groups, schools, colleges, and churches. She is a down-to-earth highly acclaimed motivational speaker and has appeared in several newspapers, magazines, on radio and television, including The Geraldo at Large Show.

Additional books can be ordered by contacting Joyce at:

www.womensempowermentseminars.com

or by emailing Joyce at joycerosemon@gmail.com

PUBLICATIONS

BY C. JOYCE FARRAR-ROSEMON

How to Be the HEAD and NOT the TAIL! A Christian Manifesto for Making Six Figures. Franklin: Providence House Publishers, 2005.

How to Get To The Palace From Your Prison! Joseph's 14 Step Program To Overcome Loneliness, Depression, discrimination, Barrenness & Abuse. Atlanta: Winner At Life Publishers, Reprint 2013.

Who Stole My Blanket? Six Easy Steps To Rebuild Your Life After An Income Loss. Atlanta: Winner At Life Publishers, 2013.

www.ingramcontent.com/pod-product-compliance
Lightning Source LLC
LaVergne TN
LVHW010934110826
845149LV00013B/2589

9780985626235